Quartet for the End of Time

ALSO BY MICHAEL SYMMONS ROBERTS

POETRY

Soft Keys
Raising Sparks
Burning Babylon
Corpus
The Half Healed
Drysalter
Selected Poems
Mancunia
Ransom

FICTION

Patrick's Alphabet
Breath

NON-FICTION

Edgelands (with Paul Farley)
Deaths of the Poets (with Paul Farley)

Quartet for the End of Time

On Music, Grief and Birdsong

MICHAEL SYMMONS
ROBERTS

JONATHAN CAPE
LONDON

13 5 7 9 10 8 6 4 2

Jonathan Cape, an imprint of Vintage, is part of the
Penguin Random House group of companies

Vintage, Penguin Random House UK, One Embassy Gardens,
8 Viaduct Gardens, London SW11 7BW

penguin.co.uk/vintage
global.penguinrandomhouse.com

First published by Jonathan Cape in 2025

Copyright © Michael Symmons Roberts 2025

Michael Symmons Roberts has asserted his right to be identified as the author of this Work in accordance with the Copyright, Designs and Patents Act 1988

Penguin Random House values and supports copyright. Copyright fuels creativity, encourages diverse voices, promotes freedom of expression and supports a vibrant culture. Thank you for purchasing an authorised edition of this book and for respecting intellectual property laws by not reproducing, scanning or distributing any part of it by any means without permission. You are supporting authors and enabling Penguin Random House to continue to publish books for everyone. No part of this book may be used or reproduced in any manner for the purpose of training artificial intelligence technologies or systems. In accordance with Article 4(3) of the DSM Directive 2019/790, Penguin Random House expressly reserves this work from the text and data mining exception.

Typeset in 10.6/15.8 pt pt Calluna by Jouve (UK), Milton Keynes
Printed and bound in Great Britain by Clays Ltd, Elcograf S.p.A.

The authorised representative in the EEA is Penguin Random House Ireland,
Morrison Chambers, 32 Nassau Street, Dublin D02 YH68

A CIP catalogue record for this book is available from the British Library

HB ISBN 9781787331853

Penguin Random House is committed to a sustainable future
for our business, our readers and our planet. This book is made
from Forest Stewardship Council® certified paper.

In memory of my parents

Contents

1	Liturgy of Crystal	1
2	Sing for the Angel who Announces the End of Time	35
3	Abyss of the Birds	74
4	Interlude	118
5	Praise to the Eternity of Jesus	147
6	Furious Dance for the Seven Trumpets	182
7	Tangle of Rainbows for the Angel who Announces the End of Time	215
8	Praise to the Immortality of Jesus	250

Bibliography   273
Acknowledgements   279

I did not in any sense want to comment upon the Apocalypse. My only wish was to articulate my desire for the dissolution of time.

Olivier Messiaen

CHAPTER 1

Liturgy of Crystal

Crystals. Liturgies. Neither conjures much for me. Diamond stylus like a mouse tooth. Meth. Wireless set. Amethyst the size of a fist, worth next to nothing. 'Liturgie de cristal' starts before dawn. Small hours between 3 and 4 a.m. The birds wake up and most of us will miss it. I have missed it. Most days I still miss it. Messiaen says you can hear a blackbird, he says you can hear a nightingale. One of each in this first movement. They improvise inside a cloud at halo-height. A blackbird has a bright, gold halo around each eye, then a soft honeycomb iris funnelling into the black hole of the pupil at the centre. In spring, there is daily eye-to-eye contact with the one outside my window. Like Elizabeth Bishop's tremendous catch in her poem 'The Fish', this blackbird has its eye on me, 'but not / to return my stare'.

—

I knew they were already gone, so I had no fear of losing them. We took a bag with the ashes of our parents in two urns and dropped them in Lake Coniston. We said a prayer and let them go. I felt nothing much. If anything, release. Then that night I woke in horror at the thought that they were drifting in the deep: dissipated, inchoate, lost and cold and drowned. It felt like those nightmares every parent has, when you take your eye off your child for a second and they vanish. Only now in reverse. I had mislaid my parents and their clouds had bloomed in water, spreading and fading as they grew. Maybe we had made a mistake. That is why people are buried in the ground. It holds them in one place. Even an urn can be interred or kept on a mantlepiece. It means there is a location, a physical trace. In water there is no regathering. But this sounds like the end of a story instead of its beginning.

—

When the composer Olivier Messiaen died in 1992 at the age of eighty-three, my first thought was that I'd missed him. I'd had it in mind, ever since I was a student, to go to Paris and sneak in at the back of the Église de la Sainte-Trinité towards the end of Sunday morning Mass. He was made organist at the church in his early twenties and held the post for the rest of his life. Reputedly, if the spirit moved him, the organ play-out at the end of Mass would turn into an extended improvisation, a free concert for all comers by one of the greatest musicians of the twentieth century.

I discovered his music by chance. As a student in the mid-1980s, I was flicking for the first time through the small classical section of my local record shop. Not my natural territory, but I was looking for something new. It was the title that grabbed me – *Quatuor pour la fin du temps* – so I bought it. On first listening, I found it decidedly strange. It was hypnotic, furious, at times ecstatic then achingly spare and still. I couldn't stop playing it. It sounded like a wild, idiosyncratic mystic modernism I hadn't heard before. It didn't seem too big a leap from some of my other listening at the time – like the Cocteau Twins and the Cure – but it opened up new imaginative spaces. The record sleeve told an amazing story about the making of this piece. He had written it while in a prisoner-of-war camp in Silesia, for the only four – rather battered – instruments available. This all added to its mystique. I tried to track down more of his music, but couldn't find much. I managed to find LPs of the *Turangalila Symphony* and a piano suite called *Vingt regards sur l'enfant-Jésus*. I loved his titles. Or rather, I loved some of them.

For each section of the *Quatuor*, Messiaen wrote an explanatory paragraph. These are by turns intense, infuriating, inspiring and downright unhelpful. Their translation from French into English no doubt blurs or skews them, but for years – and still – I can't decide if I should ignore them, try to get past them, or engage with them. Now, unable to un-read them, I find myself arguing with his explantations, jabbing at them, riffing off them. Here's a taster in English translation of Messiaen's note for the *Quartet*'s seventh section, from Anthony Pople's musicological handbook: 'I pass beyond reality and submit in ecstasy to a dizziness, a gyratory interlocking of superhuman sounds and colours. These swords of fire, these flows of blue-orange lava, these sudden stars; this is the tumult of rainbows!' The musicologist and clarinettist Rebecca Rischin in her *For the End of Time: The Story of the Messiaen Quartet* points out that some critics of the *Quartet*'s early French performances were snippy about these written statements of intent from the composer. He meant them. Every word. No critic doubted that, but some were baffled by these texts, some put off by their mystical accounts of how the music worked.

Pictured on the back cover of my first LP of *Quatuor pour la fin du temps* was a benign eccentric with thick glasses and an even thicker home-made purple scarf. The picture seemed out of kilter with the visionary power of the music. As I read about Messiaen, he intrigued me more and more. Here was a major modernist composer, teacher of many great musicians – the likes of Karlheinz Stockhausen and Pierre Boulez and Quincy Jones – drawing on musical styles and structures, rhythms and harmonies from all over the world and inventing his own. He was a Catholic visionary, an obsessive ornithologist who believed that birds had escaped or been spared the Fall, surviving intact in our wounded world. This survival included their voices, so to listen to birdsong was to hear the authentic music of Eden. If I believed that birds in the field behind our house were performing the soundtrack to Paradise each dawn then I'd get up earlier and give them more attention. If I believed it and I happened to be a composer, I'd be doing more than just listening.

—

It is not a battlefield. It is not farmed nor tended. It is not hallowed ground. It is not a place where miracles happen. It is not flat enough for games. It is not a place to walk at night. It is wasted ground. It is the first day of October. I am woken at first light, not by the sounds of Hall Hill, but by the sounds in my head, fears and losses and calculations. I hear something like a dawn chorus from the field at the end of the road. I'm not usually awake this early. I have no clue about birdsong. I reach for my phone and open the bird ID app I downloaded in the summer and have barely used. I hold it up to the window and it starts to flash up names of birds: European robin, house sparrow, Eurasian blue tit, long-tailed tit, common chaffinch, a chiding Eurasian jackdaw plus one oblivious Canada goose passing over on its way to the millpond. It's not an exotic list. But I like drawing out those names from the cloud of song, that sense of listing and codifying. It helps. At night, the sounds of the field, especially in summer with windows open, are vivid and gothic – vixen screams, dog fox hollers, colicky owls – the field, so close but never entered, has become a presence only known by sound and distant sight. It lies about ten paces from my front door, but I haven't set foot in it for years. How many years? Maybe five. Maybe more. I want to keep it that way.

In dreams about my house there is often a room I can't find but know is there. Knowing it's there is enough. I like to think Hall Hill works like that for the people in the houses that surround it. Its sounds interrupt my poems and find their way into them. The voices of the field, and my imagining of them, bled into an elegy for my dad I took three years trying to write. And the water in and under the hill seeped into the elegy for my mum which started off as a poem about the number eleven and ended up as a poem about reckoning up, about counting as a futile attempt to order grief.

Not countryside, not farmland, not urban wasteland, not wilderness, not parkland, not garden, nothing special, not even much of a hill, though there is a rise in the top left corner sufficient to see the chimney of Lowerhouse Mill and the skeletal steel drill tower at the back of the fire station. It is easier to say what Hall Hill isn't than what it is. It's a sort of brownfield, but with one foot in the greenbelt. When my sons were younger we would pick our way along the desire path by the fence – the middle of the field was too overgrown even in winter – dragging the wooden sledge too heavy to do more than sink, or the blue plastic one that shot down like a luge. As sledge-runs go it was far from precipitous but set with traps of gorse and hawthorn. In summer, the top of the rise was once a place for phone calls – good signal – decorated with crisp packets, spent lighters, crushed cans and disposable BBQ trays. Does anyone go up there now?

The one path through the north side of the field to the foot of the hill has been seized by bramble and belt-high grasses. Parts of it, always liable to floods from rainwater run-off, have become a perma-swamp. Somewhere under the swamp there used to be a metal grid. The kids would stand on it after rain (which was often, this being the north-west of England) and listen to the hollow rush of it echoing under their feet. Last time I tried to walk there, the grid itself had been swallowed by the mud. There have been makeshift efforts to restore the path, including someone dropping old wooden pallets, so with luck and good balance you could tightrope your way through. But the mud and water seized the pallets too, turned them into soggy wafers breaking with a snap when you put your weight on them. My son was one of the first to experience this, leading to a tetanus shot for a rusty nail in his foot. The climbing ropes and home-made swings of decades now hang from ash trees like swags of Spanish Moss.

—

As a window into a composer's imagination, Messiaen's short glosses on his music are fascinating. They are also wildly eccentric. He was synaesthetic, able to see sounds as colours and shapes, so his notes include phrases like 'confetti, light gemstones and colliding reflections'. As a guide to the world of the music, I find some of these descriptions oddly obstructive. One of his most beautiful pieces is a piano suite written during the Second World War called *Vingt regards sur l'enfant-Jésus*, or twenty ways of looking at (more like gazing in love at) the Christ child. One of its most radiant '*regards*', number eighteen, translates as something like 'Gaze of the Awesome Unction' (now there's a title) and the composer writes that he was inspired by an old tapestry, from which he conjures an image of Christ on horseback, wielding a gigantic sword, charging through a cloud of lightning bolts.

—

Hall Hill has been on hold forever. It is privately owned, but has been open, in theory, to everyone in the town. There have been attempts to fence off the ways in, but the fences were broken down or left incomplete. There have been planning applications, but nothing has changed to date. For the time being, it's a wild place in the middle of a town. Foxes and badgers creep out at night, make a racket in the bins, then lope back through a gap in the hedge. All this in the middle of an old mill-town but these visitors are undisturbed save by each other and the odd dog-walker. Not by us these days. There are rumours that building on the site is edging closer in spite of a campaign to stop it. The local story is that Hall Hill was the site of a dye works nearly a century back, that the soil is steeped in colours, is poisoned by them, so the cost of cleaning the ground to make it safe to build would be prohibitive. A place despoiled but protected by its own industrial past. Until recently, dyeing was one of the main trades here. You would see vans drive past with 'WE LIVE TO DYE' painted on them.

I have a friend down the road who is photographing Hall Hill in forensic detail at different times of year, collaging huge framed landscapes from multiple hyper-detailed images, every leaf, every fly on a leaf, is pin sharp if you look close enough. He has seen the field sidle into some of my poems, so he keeps asking if I want to go with him on one of his shoots. So far, there's always been a reason why I can't make the times he suggests. The truth is I won't set foot in there now. I like it kept as an imaginarium, some kind of auditory Xanadu. I'll let my friend the photographer do the forensic mapping of its ideas and projections.

LITURGY OF CRYSTAL

Trees have fallen on windy nights on Hall Hill. I thought I heard them crash, but perhaps I was only imagining what that would sound like. What I could do, inspired by the bird calls on my app, is to set up a recorder at the edge of the field and leave it switched on all night to see what it might catch.

—

He says there's a dust storm, sonic dust, I think of woodsmoke rising through the highest trees to breach the canopy. Frozen honey. Liturgy of crystal. These words are no help to me.

—

The intense, super-heated imagery of Messiaen's notes on music made more sense to me when I read his mother's work. Cécile Sauvage was a poet, and many of the words she recited to her unborn first son were from poems she wrote for him. When the composer's mother was carrying him, she would sing to him, speak to him, as many mothers do. But she also wrote a whole book of poems addressed to the soul of her unborn child. Barely any of her poems are published in English translations, but its field of imagery – the soul, the high trees, birdsong, ecstatic visions – and intensity feel rooted in the same ground as the composer's notes. Sauvage died of TB aged forty-four, cutting short a poetic career that was gaining critical acclaim and interest in her final years.

There was a lot of poetry in the Messiaen house, much of it in English. Messiaen's father, Pierre, was an English teacher and translator of Shakespeare, Blake, Milton. Cécile herself was a lover of Keats's poetry. I've had in my head for a long time a claim by Messiaen that his mother consciously 'commissioned' him before birth to become a composer, with poems written and spoken to him for that purpose. But I may have made that up. Or maybe he did. There's some myth-making in the lives of most artists, and a fair bit of it around the making of *Quartet*. Cécile and her poetry were clearly an inspiration to Olivier. However, it's Messiaen's faith, even more than his musicianship, which he claimed was gifted at birth.

Je suis né croyant – I was born believing – is a claim the composer made without caveat. I was born doubting so I find Messiaen's claim both enviable and deathly in its certainty. His family was not particularly devout, but he was. In fact, he was so devout that the words he spoke and wrote about his work never, at least in my reading of them, betray a shadow of doubt about the doctrines and texts that inspired it. He may have, must have, suffered self-doubt at points in his development as an artist, because every great artist does and Messiaen's visionary musical gifts were abundant. 'Perfect confidence is granted to the less talented as a consolation prize', as Robert Hughes pithily put it. Many artists concerned with the metaphysical in their work find it fuelled by a dialogue – at times a blazing row – between faith and doubt. Messiaen seems closer to

T. S. Eliot's favoured approach – set out in his essay on Blake – that truly innovative work comes most forcefully from an artist grounded in a theological or philosophical tradition, so they don't have to spend the work's imaginative resources constructing their own set of beliefs. The way Messiaen wrote and talked about the doctrines behind his music with absolute certainty can be a barrier to some listeners. So it was, and sometimes still is, for me. At times, what he says about his work reads like an intense kind of poetry. Sometimes it leaves me completely cold. But his music never does.

—

This smoke, this dust, this cloud above the trees will – when it clears – reveal a harmonious silence. This, says Messiaen, is heaven.

—

Quartet for the End of Time comes in eight movements. Seven is the perfect number, says the composer, so for that reason, you need eight. If you are making a work to call for the end of time, you need a final movement to enter a realm beyond the constraints of chronology into Paradise. Messiaen's fellow modernist, the British poet and artist David Jones, explained the impulse behind his own work as 'trying to make a shape out of the very things of which one is oneself made'. In Jones's case the iconography and language of the Christian faith was at the heart of it, but so was his Anglo-Welsh ancestry, the mythic matter of Britain, Roman history, shipbuilding on the River Thames and his experiences as a private soldier on the Somme. For Messiaen, alongside his faith, the things of which he was made included his mother's poetry, his deep reading of Thomas Aquinas, his fascination with the theory and instrumentation of ancient Indian music, Greek music, Japanese music and theatre, plainchant, and his obsession with birdsong. All of these play a role in his *Quartet*, but the direct source was the composer's meditation on the Book of Revelation.

—

It's the last book in the Bible, after the Old Testament, then the Gospels, the Acts of the Apostles, the various epistles to the nascent churches, then ... boom. Apocalypse. The Book of Revelation – or in full, The Revelation of St John the Divine – is based on a series of visions by an early Christian in exile on the island of Patmos for preaching his faith. It is also part of a literary tradition of apocalyptic writing which acts as a conduit between divine truths and human understanding. But crucially it offers an account to believers of the end times for those who have faith in a new heaven and a new earth. Some of its apocalyptic visions, not least the four horsemen, have cut loose from the book to become ubiquitous symbols of the end of the world. But the visionary fire at its heart has been divisive too. It was a latecomer to the biblical canon and some churches – parts of the Eastern Orthodox tradition, for example – left it out of their liturgies. Some Reformation leaders – including Martin Luther and John Calvin – expressed misgivings about the book, and it is still rare in most mainstream western churches to hear sermons on its prophecies.

For some fundamentalist believers, the visions of Revelation's author are not just accounts of totalitarian worldly powers (written under Rome's imperial rule) and God's ultimate justice. Instead, they're a coded route map to the end of the world. If you can crack the code, you can start reading international news bulletins to see how close we're getting, ticking off the signs where you spot them coming to fruition. This was not Messiaen's reading of Revelation. For him, it was not a field guide to global conflicts, but a work of beauty, a promise of a glorious world of love beyond this world, beyond the end of time.

—

The story of Messiaen's composition of *Quatuor pour la fin du temps* at the height of the Second World War and its dramatic premiere in a labour camp washroom has become a twentieth-century touchstone, a potent symbol of human strength and defiance in the face of evil, of the power of art to inspire those qualities. Musicians, Messiaen scholars and musicologists like Peter Hill, Nigel Simeone, Paul Griffiths, Christopher Dingle and Anthony Pople have opened up the making of the *Quartet*. Rebecca Rischin's work in particular – built on interviews with performers and audience members from that ice-clenched Silesian night in January 1941 – has rebalanced that story, but far from diminished it in my eyes. Understanding more about Messiaen's process of composition has deepened my admiration for the *Quartet* by making its creation believable.

From the moment I read the back-of-an-album summary when I first saw the title *Quartet for the End of Time* in a record shop, the story of the premiere was inseparable from the music. I loved the idea that a composer could be so inflamed with longing, with righteous anger and furious hope that he sat down with a blank page and a pencil to change the path of twentieth-century music. The essence of the famous story is this. A brilliant young French composer is captured during the Second World War and sent to a Nazi labour camp on the other side of Europe. Among his fellow prisoners he finds three talented musicians – a cellist called Étienne Pasquier, a clarinettist called Henri Akoka and a violinist called Jean Le Boulaire. He persuades a sympathetic guard to give him pencils and paper to write his music, so in the bitter, bleak freeze of a Silesian winter, he writes a piece for himself as pianist plus the three players he has befriended. It is a new piece in eight movements that captures their longing for liberation. Instruments were found for the players, but the cello had only three strings and the piano was a bar-room upright with some keys that stayed down when you pressed them. The only place they could perform the piece was in an unheated washroom barrack. So it was that *Quatuor*

LITURGY OF CRYSTAL

pour la fin du temps was premiered on 15 January 1941 in a camp deep in snow, to a packed audience of prisoners from many countries and professions, with their sick and injured comrades on stretchers at the front. The *Quatuor* took about an hour to perform, and though many of the prisoners had never attended a concert before, let alone one playing experimental modernist music, it was later described by the composer as the most attentive audience he had ever known.

—

This is not the book I set out to write. That other book knew its job. As books go, it was born believing. It was to be a book that mapped some territories where poetry and metaphysics cross, where the howl and the still small voice can be heard in solo and in unison. Because it would have been a kind of map, it would know where it was going when it set off towards an end as sure as Eliot's in *Four Quartets* when we will, he says, 'arrive where we started / And know the place for the first time'. But then I started writing and the words kept looping back to the loss of my dad just before before the pandemic, then my mum during. When the world contracted – for most of us – to the measure of our walls I tried to work my way back into the right book. But the words began to form into poems instead. I returned to my original maps for this book (disguised as book proposals) and they no longer made sense to me. It put me in mind of Philip Larkin's lament that 'you don't write the poems you really want to write' because 'the words somehow refuse to come'.

What I did have was a title. It was Messiaen's title, translated into English. *Quartet for the End of Time* still made sense to me. I saw a way in through the idea of ends, of apocalypse in its sense as a place, a time or an idea in which a revelation or encounter with God might take place. Maybe. That took me back to Messiaen's starting point for his *Quartet* – the Book of Revelation, Chapter 10. The first time I ever heard or read that passage was on the sleeve of that Messiaen LP. I remember the angel more than anything, the sheer scale of it:

> And I saw another mighty angel come down from heaven, clothed with a cloud: and a rainbow was upon his head, and his face was as it were the sun, and his feet as pillars of fire: And he had in his hand a little book open: and he set his right foot upon the sea, and his left foot on the earth, And cried with a loud voice, as when a lion roareth: and when he had cried, seven thunders uttered their voices. And when the seven thunders had uttered their voices, I was about to write: and I heard a voice from heaven saying unto me, Seal up those things which the seven thunders uttered, and write them not.

—

Saturday morning in early autumn. For the first time in months there is a bite to the air. As ever when we pull up outside, my parents have been watching for us. I've got the boot open and I'm lifting out Mum's birthday present for next week – I forget what we gave her now – and a bag of small gifts and cards from their grandsons. My dad walks up next to me and offers to help take the stuff in. It's fine, no, don't worry. He kisses me on the top of my head as he has at every arrival or departure scene for as long as I can remember. I reach into the bag, murmuring something about the rude jokes on the cards from the boys, and I take out a copy of a book of poems called *Mancunia*. It was newly published and they were going to buy some copies but I said I'd bring them some instead. He looks at the cover and I tell him there's a poem in it with a title that might give him a start, but it's just a dream I had, don't worry. He looks quizzical. You'll find it, don't worry. I just thought I ought to say something before you come across it. It was just a dream I had. A nightmare. There you go.

Truth is I had been dreading this for weeks, whether to mention the poem or not say anything and hope he doesn't read it. They never talk about my poems, so it will pass unnoticed. Even this time, when I felt I had to flag up one title, I know he will never mention it. And I will never ask. He tucks the book under his arm and we walk in, he says we should go to the pub for lunch, a drink. That's great. Let's do it. Truth is that it wasn't just a single dream, but loops and loops of it for weeks. Always the same.

—

QUARTET FOR THE END OF TIME

MY FATHER'S DEATH

I don't believe in omens,
but that wedding bowl in smithereens,
then the starling in our hallway
whose fear sent the dog into a fury,

then those cast-in-blue recurrent dreams
in which he visits me and seems
aware of some unspoken threat
from which I wake in dread, *and yet*,

and yet he is still here, *thank God*. Am I
dry-running for that day,
as if to preview loss might stem its force,
and so he goes, and goes, and goes?

I need to break its hold.
I set a trap, an apple iced with mould,
heavy with its sick perfume:
open window, north-facing room.

I sit in wait and watch it land:
my father's death, close up, new-spawned
or rather, hatched,
so purposeful in dreams, now, watched,

can barely hold its line in air,
I speak out loud an ancient prayer
I only half-believe
and on the *s* of *save*

it flutters to my hand and look,
its iridescent jet, its wings of black lacework,
the hidden kernel of a rose,
a gothic wind-up toy. I close

my fist on it, too slow, it's gone.
You parasite, you origami con,
you blow-in, mayfly, duff lit spill,
now go, and never come again. *I know you will.*

—

Visionary or nonsense. All the noise surrounding the *Quartet* makes it inconceivable as a soundtrack to stick on in the background while you're queueing for a drive-thru or worrying about your overdraft. You won't be whistling it in the street, unless you're a bird. Part of that surrounding noise is the composer's account of its inspiration, themes and scriptural sources, its reputation as a work of mystical power. The noise also includes the story of the premiere with its message of resilience and hope at one of the twentieth century's bleakest moments. Visionary is a word to be wary of, especially when applied to an artist, but in this case it's hard to avoid. *Quartet* evokes a vision of the future, but it's a future that lies beyond death, beyond time, beyond any aspect of this world.

Messiaen was literally visionary too. His synaesthesia meant seeing sounds not just as static colours, but a dazzling, shifting kaleidoscope, which he explained in notes to accompany his compositions. The list he attached to a later piece called 'Colours of the Celestial City' includes the sounds of yellow topaz, red stained with blue, mauve, amethyst, violet, orange, sapphire, milky-white, grey, rose and emerald. I've always found these colour guides to music read like exotic standalone poems, albeit adding nothing whatsoever to my ears-only reception of his work. When you factor in his belief that birdsong is the unfallen music of Eden, and his claim that the *Quartet* contains passages of song transcribed from blackbirds and nightingales, it's not hard to see how some listeners might – and do – find it all a bit much.

As not just a visionary but a groundbreaking modernist innovator, Messiaen was impossible to ignore for the generation of composers who followed him, many of whom were taught by him too. The composer James MacMillan, with whom I've collaborated many times as a librettist, told me that some of Messiaen's acolytes and pupils – while acknowledging the power, originality and importance of his music, not to mention being influenced by it in their own work – found his whole visionary project discomforting, maybe even lacking in taste. Some regarded his mystical modernism to be too garish, too heavy with the scent of incense, a taint of Catholic tat like the musical equivalent of plastic statues sold at grottos. One critic cited by Rebecca Rischin, in his review of the 1945 premiere of Messiaen's cantata *Trois Petite Liturgies de la Présence Divine* (written during the war, shortly after the completion of the *Quartet*) described it as 'tinsel, false magnificence and pseudo-mysticism', crowning his review with an image of the work as a flabby angel wearing lipstick, with dirty nails and clammy hands. But Jean Cocteau, at the same premiere, reportedly declared it a work of genius, and the 'flabby angel' critic went on to be a Messiaen enthusiast.

It's not that Messiaen couldn't write the hard-core 'nothing-but-the-dots-on-the-page' stuff. Serialism is a set of musical tools using fixed series of notes to generate patterns, breaking out of traditional notions of harmony. Messiaen's 1949 piece *Mode de valeurs et d'intensités* (*Modes of Values, Durations and Intensities*) was, says James, 'a kind of exercise in complete, total serialism. It's not just the twelve pitches that are serialised, he serialises everything. He was the first to do that and found it interesting for a time, then abandoned it.' Though he never lost his fascination with patterns and sequences and loops, Messiaen's music arose from powerful beliefs, visions and emotions. Too powerful for some. He described his *Turangalila Symphony* as an expression of unbounded, expansive joy. But when it was premiered the same year, some of his contemporaries likened it to the music of a bordello or, even worse in their eyes, to film music. There is a panoramic sweep to it, a cinematic quality heightened by the other-worldly swoop of the ondes martenot, an electronic instrument developed by Maurice Martenot, a former radio operator in the First World War, inspired by the shifting tones of military radio oscillators. It went on to feature in sci-fi soundtracks, but its place in orchestral music was secured by Messiaen. I love the fact that the one-eyed spaceship pilot heroine of Matt Groening's animation *Futurama* – Turanga Leela – was named after Messiaen's expansive 'hymn to joy'. Experimental, mystical, often intensely emotive, Messiaen's music is a heady mix. 'Crime of crimes', says James, 'it touches the heart.'

—

I can understand why Monsieur Martenot was captivated by the overlapping tones of his army radios. Even now, a de-tuned radio can capture snatches of Morse code, rasping phone-in rants, intros to songs so distorted you can't make out the language. And when they drift, you can hear the radio waves, an ether full of voices washing into and through each other. *Ondes* in French translates to waves – Martenot's waves. His military kit would, like most early radio equipment, rely on a crystal to pull these waves out of the air. Some sets used several different crystals – iron pyrites (fools' gold), white lead, carborundum, phosphor bronze – to allow switching between them in search of a stronger signal.

—

'Liturgie de cristal', the *Quartet*'s first movement, is short. Two minutes and sixteen seconds in the version I'm listening to now. But other versions stretch to a languid three minutes. That's the trouble with time – musical or theological – it's hard to nail down. The recording of the *Quartet* I've got on now is the first, from 1956. It was recorded, perhaps fittingly, in a former Benedictine monastery in Paris's Latin Quarter, now home to the Schola Cantorum, an historic conservatoire with Messiaen on its roll of celebrated teachers. Étienne Pasquier, who played the cello in the *Quartet*'s famous premiere, was joined for the recording by his violinist brother Jean and the clarinettist André Vacellier. What makes it unique is the fact that the composer himself was playing piano and presiding. Since he was part of it, it's tempting to regard this recording as definitive. In terms of tone, dynamic range and expression, it must be 'authentic', as Pasquier put it. The odd thing to me, as a listener, is that it seems out of kilter with some of the composer's own instructions on tempo. Some more recent recordings seem to my ears, ironically, better at the time thing than his own recording. I assumed this meant my hearing, not the music, must be out of kilter, but some musicologists – including Rebecca Rischin – while referring to this as 'a superlative recording', point out that several movements are played slower than indicated on the score, another at nearly twice the pace called for, and this first movement 'Liturgie de cristal' 'is somewhat unsteady, and at times the ensemble is out of sync'. Nonetheless, I love this recording and it's become one of a pair I go back to again and again.

For a movement with a title as static as this one, 'Liturgy of Crystal' is rapid, whichever the recording. It's birds-a-go-go from the opening bar. When I first put it on in my student room I remember finding it so weird that I grabbed my headphones so I could listen in private until I'd worked out exactly what the hell it was. All my reference points for chamber music – of which there were not many – were stately, refined. I thought of period dramas, polite and gloved applause, chairs with velvet cushions. But this one was like sticking my head into a surreal aviary in which the birds sound like they've eaten too much fermented fruit. It's not just one bird either, all the instruments are at it. There was no turning back.

—

When I think of a crystal liturgy, the words not the music, and imagine what it might look like, I imagine a church full of sun pouring in from high windows, worshippers transfigured into precious stone, multicoloured, shaping and changing the light as it passes through each to the other. As pictures go, it's static, which clearly isn't what Messiaen had in mind, judging by this pacy romp I'm listening to on loop. The church in my imagined scene of a petrified Mass is set in Paris, but not because Messiaen lived there.

A couple of years before I stumbled upon the *Quartet*, I had gone to Paris with my family. I was in my late teens. I'm sure my plan was to hang out on the Left Bank smoking Gitanes and pretending to be a musician, but my parents were keen to do the top ten places from the guidebook so we went to the Sainte-Chapelle. All I knew was that it was an old church, so I can't say it was high on my list at the time. But it should have been. It has one of the world's great collections of stained glass. I remember it, essentially, as a majestic, kaleidoscopic glasshouse. On the day we went, there was a low autumn slant to the sun so we were walking on jewels. Messiaen visited too, at the age of eleven. Already a composer and a born believer, he recalled it as an intense and overwhelming experience of colour. The difference is, he could hear the colours too.

—

I have to switch off 'Liturgie de cristal'. It's too frenetic. Listening on loop is driving up my blood pressure. This seems at odds with the temperature of crystal in the early chapters of Revelation, a frozen ocean described as glassy, crystalline, leading up to the heavenly throne. There are more crystals in the later chapters too, when the New Jerusalem appears, its city walls studded with jasper, sapphire, agate, emerald, onyx, ruby, chrysolite, beryl, topaz and amethyst.

There's an old black-and-white photograph of Messiaen with his collection of crystals. He knew his gems. It looks like a serious collection, with some samples the size of his head arranged on glass shelves. His descriptions of his own music in terms of colours makes his shelves of semi-precious stones a kind of sound library. I have one of my own. But mine consists of audio files, some from my previous work as a radio producer, to draw from if a project ever required the sound of a busy street in Manchester, or church bells in Vienna, or a blackbird singing in a square in Berlin. I left my job as a producer twenty years ago, though writing and talking on radio is still part of my work.

I collect recordings for my sound library, but I never – or very rarely – listen back to them, and now I work with producers who have their own sound libraries and don't need mine. But I carry a recorder in my bag wherever I go. If I'm caught without it and something comes up – a metro station announcement in a foreign city, or a new chant at the football – I'll catch it on my phone. Everything gets digitally labelled and filed in categories. There is literally no point to this.

—

If there is a heaven I want noise in it. Not just the noise of us, but all the birds, all the fish, insects, plants. I want to hear the trees, not just the winds that play in them.

—

In 1939, as the German armies swept across Europe, Messiaen received his call-up. He was already what would now be described as an emerging artist. Followers of contemporary composition would know his name and some of his work. He was declared medically unfit for active combat, so was assigned to a group of orderlies supporting medics in the field. He could see sounds as colours, colours as sounds. He could see a world beyond the end of time. But he wore spectacles as thick as welding goggles. He failed the medical on poor vision.

He was already married to Claire Delbos, a composer and violinist, and they had a young son, Pascal. Messiaen knew he would miss both of them terribly as long as he was away. He did manage to smuggle a handful of pocket orchestral scores in his army backpack, including some Bach, Stravinsky, Debussy and Berg. Even if his military duties made it impossible to create his own music, he would immerse himself in the music of others on the page. Although he was still months from capture and transit to the labour camp in Silesia, he already had versions of two sections for *Quartet* in previous incarnations, but neither of them was the frantic 'Liturgie de cristal' which opens the piece. One more movement – 'Abyss of the Birds', the third – was about to be created before he left France, though as yet there was no sign of *Quatuor pour la fin du temps*.

—

As a connoisseur of birdsong, Messiaen paid particular attention to the dawn chorus, not just in France but later at the camp in Görlitz, in the streets around his Paris apartment, at his rural retreat – Pétichet on the banks of the Lac de Laffrey in Isère – and wherever he travelled in his long globe-trotting career as a composer. If this chorus is the sound of the sacred, then it makes sense to pay it due attention as Messiaen does. Dawn, in books of hours, is not the start of the canonical day. There have already been several liturgies long before first light. But lauds is the first true daytime liturgy, marked with psalms of praise for the risen sun and the risen God. The equivalent in poetry is the aubade, a daybreak poem celebrating love but often with the undertow of nights of passion ending and lovers parting. John Donne's twist on the aubade in 'The Sunne Rising' – tell the sun to get back in its box so I can stay with my lover – or Philip Larkin's in his 'Aubade' – the lover is death and it's coming for me – are the kinds of feint that keep these forms alive.

I've never knowingly written an aubade. Maybe I stay up too late. Although I have been getting up much earlier to write this book. The house is quieter and that makes it easier for the connections to come. I wake up in a bedroom at the front of the house eavesdropping on Hall Hill and go straight to my desk in a bedroom at the back facing north towards the glass and steel stalagmites of Manchester. I have it in mind one day to record the dawn chorus on Hall Hill. But I can't work out how. If I am to capture the song as it wakes me some mornings, then I can't just walk into the field with a recorder. That's too close, not at all how I hear it when it wakes me up. Maybe I should set up a microphone outside my window. The whole point of the field for me is that I don't go in it. It will take a bit of thought. And the right microphone. But every time I think about it I loop back to the fact that there's no point to it. Am I going to listen to it every now and then? No. Could it be useful for some future research or performance or project? No. It's all available online in much higher quality than I could capture.

—

Among the carefully catalogued files I don't open in my sound library is a series of short voicemail messages, several from my dad to my mobile just checking in, asking how we all are, ending each with an audible 'what can you do?' shrug at how long it's taking for the engineer to come round to fix our landline, which has been down for days. He is worried that it leaves us cut off from the world, even though he has our mobile numbers and my parents are the only people who ever call us on the landline. I have five of these messages, of varying lengths between ten seconds and a minute, left on my phone over the course of a week or two. I called him back after each message, but for some reason I kept the recordings on my phone. Now I'm glad to have them, filed under his initials in the sound library. There are a lot of files I never open since I have no need to hear them. These five files were kept for the keeping, never the listening.

    There were two messages on the landline voicemail too, left the day before his sudden death, saying hello, it's only me, nothing urgent, just seeing how you all are. No rush to call back. And we were busy in the day and out last night and didn't rush to call back, then were woken first thing by a call from Mum at sixes and sevens calling my number instead of my sister's to splutter 'I think your dad has died in the night.' I live ninety minutes' drive away and my sister lives round the corner. I get dressed and straight in the car as Mum calls my sister. On the motorway I am going over and over the call, because the phrase 'I think your dad has died...' has a crack in it. Maybe he was just very deeply asleep. Maybe he's passed out. He's not a good sleeper so perhaps that caught up with him. Maybe when she put the phone down on me but before she dialled my sister she heard him calling and her saying I thought you had gone and him scoffing then annoyed that she had worried us and telling her to call back but at home they say he's in the car on his way to you so they don't want to call when I'm driving but it's all fine and I'll know that when I get there. He is an ex-smoker, a drinker of Scotch since he learnt to drink doing national service, a cancer survivor for more than a decade.

A white flash in the mirror. A car doing twice my speed manifests in an instant then cuts right into the outside lane, too close to me, then does the same to a van and cuts back in front of me, then undertakes the van, swings out and loses it, clips the crash barrier and drifts. Everyone is braking, but it's over in a second and he's sitting – a young guy in a white Mercedes – parked up on the hard shoulder and staring out through the windscreen, the car and him apparently untouched. Was it my fault? Did he clip the back of my car and that distracted him, was I going too slow, too fast? I was – in both senses – miles away. None of this is my fault. But I hadn't called Dad back this week and that was. I was short with him earlier in the week when he called to tell me a joke and I was stressed and running late and it wasn't the best joke and he could probably tell I was wound up. I should pull over and check the back of the car to see if there's a white mark from the Mercedes meaning I should have stopped if there was contact so I stop and there isn't one and I knew there was no contact. I think. She said I think. By the time I get there it will be clear. One way or the other. And those messages on the voicemail will mean nothing or everything. A missed chance for a final conversation, a better one. Something or nothing.

—

Looking back over my notes for the poem 'My Father's Death' I remembered I had made a last-minute cut before it went to print. The last two stanzas had always read:

> it flutters to my hand and look,
> its iridescent jet, its wings of black lacework,
> the hidden kernel of a rose,
> a gothic wind-up toy. I close

> my fist on it, too slow, it's gone.
> You parasite, you origami con,
> you blow-in, mayfly, duff lit spill,
> now go, and never come again. *I know you will.*

In the final proofs for my collection *Mancunia* I deleted the last stanza and changed 'I close' in the previous stanza to 'so close', so the poem as published in *Mancunia* ends on a close brush with my father's death, rather than a failed attempt to trap it, then a declaration of certainty that it would return.

This eleventh hour cut seems crazy to me now. It was made with one reader in mind. I couldn't face the idea of Dad reading the final phrase '*I know you will*', as if there was something shocking in my poem declaring that he was mortal. The certainty of it. The fact of his son declaring it in public. As if writing him a poem called 'My Father's Death' wasn't bad enough.

—

I have a new picture in mind now when I listen to the *Quartet*'s first movement. 'Liturgie de cristal' meant nothing to me when I first heard the music, not having any interest in crystals or liturgies. It sounded like a contradiction, a liturgy as a ritual people perform in unison, and a crystal as a lump of something ancient that once contained life but is now rock hard, albeit colourful. It sounds 'spiritual', which puts me in mind of a line from Anne Carson's 'On Snow': 'A sort of dreariness, like a heavy smell of coats, comes down on the word "spiritual" and makes religion impossible for me.'

That dreariness is in my head when I think of the words 'Liturgy of Crystal', though 'Liturgie de cristal' does sound more enticing, I admit. It suggests to me a music both stately and solemn. Ancient too. Something earnest to be said and done in church. The *Quartet*'s first movement is not like this at all. But the ideas behind 'liturgy' are more interesting than the word itself. I like the notion that human beings are liturgical animals (as well as metaphysical animals, but that's for later) and we can't help but make these rituals. The philosopher Catherine Pickstock uses the word liturgy to explore patterns of behaviour in secular as well as religious culture. She suggests that we don't just enact liturgies to practise what we already believe, but that by practising them we believe what they inculcate. A Sunday morning walk to the shop to buy the papers or a walk down the road to go to Mass may both make me feel apocalyptic, but perhaps with a different end result. If liturgy can be applied to any repeated ritual or practice, then I guess poems could be seen as 'liturgies' too. They can be incantatory, thrive on repetition, lend themselves to being learnt by heart. Like any liturgy, they can be liturgies of profundity and joy, or empty ones, or both. For all that, I'm afraid the word still leaves me cold.

—

When I was reading about Görlitz, the half-German, half-Polish town with a foot on each side of the River Neisse, the site of the Nazi labour camp where the *Quartet*'s legendary premiere took place, I found out Messiaen wasn't the only visionary to have lived there. It was the home of the seventeenth-century mystic Jakob Böhme, whose visions and revelations brought him into conflict with the religious authorities of his day, and whose writings have fascinated not just believers and seekers (especially those in the Lutheran tradition) but also poets including Blake, Yeats and Coleridge. His essay 'Life Beyond the Senses' takes the form of a dialogue between teacher and student, including an attempt to describe the end of time. Böhme does believe in a bodily life after death, but not the flesh, gristle, veins and muscles we have now. Our bodies have been damaged and weakened by the Fall. Resurrection bodies will, he says, be crystalline and translucent, so the divine light will shine through us unimpeded. No shadows in heaven. No genders either. He believes those came with the Fall, and will be gone after the end of time. It will be full of light and joy, he says, this place where everything and everyone is crystal clear.

CHAPTER 2

Sing for the Angel who Announces the End of Time

Shout, sing, howl for the angel who declares the end of time. The music of this second movement is bookended. It's around four minutes long and there's a fast, short picture at the top and end of the piece conjuring – according to the composer's notes – that mighty angel telling us time's up. And how formidable that angel is, with one foot on the sea and one foot on the earth, so tall that most of his body is cloaked in cloud and a rainbow on his brow like a diadem. The two short bookend sections stand strong to hold between them a passage of music so measured and sinuous it sounds like it was written as a crazy-fast passage now being played deliberately too slowly so new players can learn their parts. This middle section, Messiaen says, evokes the songs of the air, the sky's own harmonics. He points out the blue-orange chords, but as always his colour notes mean nothing to me, save wishing I could see sounds as colours like he could. He talks about the plainchant of the violin and cello juxtaposed with the chimes of the piano. I hear the chimes. The piano as a tolling bell is not as vivid here as in later movements. Above all, this second movement is cinematic for me, its opening like a tilt up to reveal the scale of this towering angel – foot to diadem – then in the middle section the water dripping from his outstretched arms and the birds circling around his head in celebration, as if he's risen up from the seabed. Now I'm thinking of a film camera, that mighty angel shades into Gulliver, King Kong. Not helpful. Jakob Böhme wrote that we should move beyond mental images as they misdirect us from the truth. But he never saw *King Kong*.

—

I can't help but think of the pub landlady calling time in *The Waste Land*, a referee's whistle in extra time, so inexplicably late that the whole stadium is whistling. And I wonder about the declaration, the calling, the exact moment of the end of time. A particular word, maybe, that enacts it. Then we find ourselves in timelessness. We do not know the day or the hour. As the gospel song warns – keep your lamps trimmed and burning. But the end of time is a vast steel door, impossible to see through, round, over. The very act of thinking about it takes place in time, as does the waiting for it. At the point where the angel calls it, all the clocks stop but so does everything – birth, death, speech, thought, despair, love, passion, compassion, fear, hope . . . all are impossible to conceive outside time. At least for me they are. Maybe if I had a stronger faith in something beyond the end of time I would be able to imagine some kind of individual existence there.

I can begin to conceptualise a life after this one, some kind of afterlife that means a new world with all the physicality and sensuality and complexity and variety of this one. I'm not interested in a disembodied soup of souls. Böhme's see-through crystal bodies appeal to me as poetry, but I can't imagine what it would be like to be such a body. If there is to be a life beyond the end of this one, I'm drawn to the bodily visions, more like Stanley Spencer's weirdly unsettling but joyful Cookham resurrection paintings with people rising from their graveyard plots and brushing the soil from their coats. I'm even more drawn to visions like Kate Wilson's paintings of the risen life as a wide sweep of stairs that could be the way up from a station on the Jubilee or Northern Lines, where people stop to greet and embrace as they step out blinking into their reborn city.

—

Messiaen believed that time was not absolute, but a part of God's creation. It only keeps moving because God wants it to keep moving. So when the world's time is up, we need to be ready for it. The trouble is, we haven't a clue how much time we have left. The roots of the word 'waiting' lie in watchfulness, wakefulness, a kind of vigilance: what Simone Weil called 'attention'. If Advent is a provocation, to contemplate the future rather than to make a headlong dash for it, to live in the present with the edge of fragility that makes it vivid and precious, then that's worth practising. Perhaps then we can recover, as Patrick Kavanagh put it in his poem 'Advent', 'the newness that was in every stale thing / when we looked at it as children'. Seen through that lens, winter nights spent on railway station platforms are more than character-building. They are soul-building.

It's a vexed question, how to wait for the end of time. The *Quartet*'s composer exemplifies the devotional model – a patient inner preparedness. In fact, he outstrips that model with his active longing for the clock to stop. I have spent most of my life employing the opposite approach, seeing signs of personal and global finitude in every headline or symptom, as if the act of foreseeing the end is the best way to forestall it. At some level, I must believe that 'it' – fate, apocalypse, disaster – wants you to stop worrying about it, to become blasé and get on with your apparently limitless life, then it will come when you are looking in the other direction. This pointless vigilance may be a cause or an effect of writing poems, but I know a lot of poets who do it.

—

Julia Margaret Cameron, the pioneering Victorian portrait photographer of, among other luminaries, Alfred Lord Tennyson (himself not averse to catastrophising) and Charles Darwin, made some of the weirdest images I know on the subject of eschatological waiting. Inspired by the gospel story of the wise and foolish bridesmaids, she assembled five young women – three called Mary and two whose names are now forgotten – and dressed them for a pair of staged images, looking wise in one and foolish in the other. In Matthew's gospel, the ten bridesmaids are waiting for the bridegroom to arrive to take them into the wedding. Five, not knowing how long they will be waiting, take spare oil to keep their lamps burning. The other five, when their lamps burn out, have to go to buy some more. Big mistake. While they are away the bridegroom turns up and by the time they are back he has taken the wise five bridesmaids into the wedding and shut the door behind him. The takeaway from this is that end-of-time vigilance is not a waste of time if it's pointed in the right direction. In fact, if you let it slip, you will miss out on eternity.

Cameron's prints are distressed. Her wise bridesmaids look like they are standing in a pool of fog, while the foolish are peppered with snow and ash from the waist down. In both images, some faces are out of focus. But the bridesmaids do not look distressed at all. A bit pensive, perhaps, but given that they are acting out a parable of the end of time, they look remarkably unencumbered by the thought of it. The accompanying notes to the pictures – held by the Victoria and Albert Museum – point to one contemporary critic's observation that the two sets of bridesmaids look as foolish as each other, with their faux first-century garb and lamps (or lack of), but to me they don't look foolish, just sad and static. Even the wise ones look in two minds about the wedding. I'm with them. Not in their wisdom, but in their equivocation.

—

To approach the end of this world with a single-minded longing, as Messiaen did, may be a sign of wisdom and of powerful faith, but it looks like a kind of madness. In my decades of listening to the *Quartet*, there have been gaps. Some as long as a year or two. But it's never the music itself that puts me off. It's the vision behind it. At times I wish there was at least a flicker of a sense of loss at the idea that time, and this world, are about to be stopped in their tracks. This music was conceived at a moment of historic suffering and hopelessness by a composer in a labour camp across the continent from home. Except some of it wasn't. It's complicated. As is my love of the *Quartet*. It has been part of my adult life in a way no other single piece of music has. But sometimes it makes me feel faithless, or hopeless, unflinching in my longing for this world to keep the next world at arm's length.

—

When I got to the house the sliver of light in the 'I think' phrase had vanished. Because he was gone. A policewoman was sitting on the sofa talking to Mum about his sudden death. Because it was unexpected there were protocols. My sister was with Mum and they were trying to hold each other together. The ambulance arrived to take the body away. They said they would wait five minutes for me to go up and pay my respects first. I must have hesitated for a second because my sister said 'you should'. Upstairs was the small back bedroom set up with a TV and chair, where he would go on sleepless nights, which meant most nights. Near the landing, I held back between steps, trying to find some steel to walk into the presence of him-and-not-him. In life, his was the calmest presence I knew. Now I didn't want to stand in the same room.

When I did go in, I spoke to him, though I wondered if it made sense to do so. I knew he wasn't there. I said the things I would have told him if I'd had the chance. I kissed him on the forehead – waxy, no warmer than the room. All the details of his insomniac routine were in place – the chair pushed up close to the TV always set to rolling news on Al Jazeera, the glass of Bell's whisky unfinished on the windowsill next to his chair, a joke book next to it. And him in dark red pyjamas and a thin blue cotton dressing gown. I remember standing in front of him, crossing myself, not knowing how to measure this moment nor how to bring it to a close. It would be the last time I would ever see this, him, but wherever he was now it was a long, long, long way from here.

—

It takes a cast of thousands to hold one person's past in place. He held most of it, of course, until he left that body. But my mum held some of it, and my sister and me, the grandchildren, his friends here and his colleagues from past episodes: his national service in Egypt, his job in the sales department at Tootal Textiles in Manchester where he met Mum who was the boss's secretary, his contacts in the factories around Trafford Park when he was working as a sales rep selling cardboard boxes, then later as a manager, a life in sales meant meeting so many people and they all held some of it. His diaries, listing meetings, are in boxes in the garage. It takes a large, disparate, dispersed collection of witnesses to hold his past in place. Many, most, of them are gone. I wish I'd recorded interviews with him, talking through his life decade by decade. The day he died was 11/11, Remembrance Day. As I drove back through the glory of iced fields and bare trees I stopped thinking about what I wished I'd told him and started listing what I would have asked him in that interview.

There was nothing unusual about the manner of his dying. In many ways it was a perfect way to go – in his eighties, in the night, at home. We think he went in his sleep, but Mum felt bad in case he called out and she hadn't heard him. He always said he expected to go sooner, so his last decade or so felt like a bonus. As a friend of mine said of his own dad's death in old age: 'I didn't want him to live forever, just a bit longer.' He was not a man of faith, nor an atheist. He was a fatalist, almost to the point where anything was 'probably for the best'. I don't know where he is now. Not here nor there. The Christian view of the afterlife behind the *Quartet* holds that the next world is yet to come, at a point in history (the end and consummation of it) signalled in Revelation by the angel with a trumpet in Messiaen's second movement. It won't be some ethereal existence but more intensely physical than this one, the earth remade, not clouds and harps. So the dead, as they wait for time to be called, are in a halfway house, a holding place. The theologian N. T. Wright says the early Christians believed in a two-step notion of life after death. The biblical promise of 'many mansions' rests on a translation into 'mansions' of a Greek word for a temporary resting place, a traveller's rest. I find it hard not to get too concrete about this idea, imagining it as a motorway service station on the M6 just north of Birmingham. Hilton Park, in fact, where Dad used to stop on family trips to visit our grandparents. I don't think he imagined being there for eternity, though I can imagine being there might lead to a longing for the angel to announce the end of time.

—

This is the trouble with thinking about the end of time and what might come before and after it. The metaphors come crashing down like stage flats as soon as you set them up. None of them will do. That's why Messiaen's metaphorical, Revelation-inflected descriptions of the *Quartet*'s eight movements are as unhelpful as they are (sometimes) beautiful. The music, however, like the birds in the third movement, can go right up to the end of time and beyond it, without falling flat.

—

Between is an interesting place to be: between places, times, states of being. That's why so much art and literature is set there: caught between two lovers, torn between desire and duty, lost between two nations, two worlds, two lives. Between means border country, edgelands, disputed territory where lawlessness is rife and frontiers porous. There's an inherent creative tension in waiting, whether it's for the ghost of Hamlet's father, or the dawn of Henry V's battle, or Romeo's arrival, or (famously undermining all this waiting) Godot. Or on a platform at Crewe Station in December.

One month on from losing Dad, heading back north from London, and the trains are screwed. Again. Cancellations, delays. The sign above the platform says there may be one last shot at getting home before they shut down for the night. I'm sure I am forgetting things about him and his life. Or rather, his life is breaking into episodes. I am making notes for a poem about him, but that is breaking into episodes too. I can't hold him together in my head. He has let his past go. The thread that holds it all together – as much as the past can be held – is the continuing presence of a person in a body, getting up each morning, marking the days, holding back the end of time.

—

What to make of this mighty, cinematic angel in the second movement? Messiaen's title sounds like an imperative – 'Vocalise, pour l'Ange qui annonce la fin du temps'. To my mind the title points at us, the listeners, not the players. Sure, the instruments in this movement sing, maybe cry out in places. He says the start and finish of this section are depictions of the angel, while the middle evokes the harmonies of the sky. Maybe it's not just us being asked to vocalise for this angel. Maybe it's the whole of creation, a kind of *lacrimae rerum* but instead of 'the tears of things', this is 'the songs of things'.

I never had much time for angels. Or at least, I couldn't get past the kitsch, the Christmas cards and saccharine songs. Then along came Wim Wenders. Well, it wasn't only Wim Wenders, but the release of the German director's fantasy *Wings of Desire* in the late 1980s certainly helped to shift my perspective. I was first drawn to the film because I'd read it was influenced by Rainer Maria Rilke's poetry, and in particular his mysterious, terrifying angels in the *Duino Elegies*. These were more like Messiaen's mighty angels, the terror they inspire born out of their unimaginable beauty. Since I was already fascinated by Rilke, I decided to give the film a go.

I was in my early twenties at the time, still nominally an atheist, and I was not 'in a good place', as they say. I was stuck in the wrong job, in the wrong city, in a rented box room in a shared house. I couldn't afford to go out, and knew no one there to go out with. I'd had episodes of depression since childhood – like my mum and her dad – but this was a particularly bad one. It's not an unfamiliar story, and I knew I was more fortunate than many. But it put me in a state of uncertainty and questioning. So one night, finding it by chance while flicking through channels, I watched *Wings of Desire* through the blizzard on the screen of my black and white portable TV. It's a classic now, and led to many imitations. But at the time it seemed new.

What it depicts is an angel, wonderfully played by Bruno Ganz, who chooses to make a slow and painful descent into becoming earthly, becoming mortal. He falls in love with one of us mortals, a trapeze artist no less, and sacrifices the safe world of the immortals to step into ours, from eternity to our broken, beautiful mortality. The angel wants to be fully alive, and to be fully alive means risk, woundedness, pain and loss, but he knows this is the price of love, of self-giving, of beauty.

Something about that film got to me. Wim Wenders's angels were a nod to the angels of Rilke, and sent me back to them. Rilke was no conventional religious believer, but his poems – like Messiaen's music – are mystical and radical and so intense they should probably require a prescription to read them. His ten *Duino Elegies*, written in fits and starts between 1912 and 1923, open with a cry that translates to something like: 'Who, if I cry out, will hear me among the ranks of angels?' The film – and my return to Rilke's poems – didn't amount to a Damascene moment, but they were important steps, struggling as I was towards a different kind of faith, no longer able to muster belief in my atheism.

—

Before Messiaen, my only encounters with the end of time in films and books were grim, and tended to militate against the idea of waiting for it with anything but dread. The fantastic subtlety and emotional range of Messiaen's vision, combined with the poetic power of his subtitles (one movement called 'Furious Dance for the Seven Trumpets', another 'Abyss of the Birds') made a big impression on me. I was struck by the ordinariness with which he described (in sleeve notes) the extraordinary events of the end of time: angels bestriding oceans, trumpets sounding. The fact that the *Quartet* was written when Messiaen was a prisoner of war only served to heighten the power of the piece, though Messiaen himself stressed that he was not driven by despair at the state of this world, just a simple and genuine longing for the next one.

Later, working as a documentary film-maker, I found myself still circling round these ideas. Travelling through the Southern states of America with a colleague, Iwan Russell-Jones, making a BBC radio series about apocalyptic theology and its influence on politics, culture, morality, I met people who believed with utter certainty that the apocalyptic clock was ticking, and that the signs were there for all to read. The coming of the cashless society was a sign of the end times, apparently (we may have got away with that one so far), as was, more disturbingly, peace-making of various kinds, notably in the Middle East. I met people who claimed that the Antichrist was one of several real-life politicians (usually in Europe) duping us all before plunging us into the final catastrophe leading to the Second Coming.

I'd go back to my hotel room and conclude they were insane, while barely admitting the sliver of fear that they might, just might be right. Then I'd switch on the TV and see the mainstream news channels talking a pretty good apocalypse themselves, be it disease or famine or global war. In the Christian tradition, the season of Advent – leading up to the incarnation – offers a more familiar, less toxic way of looking towards the end of time. If Advent means anything today it means waiting for Christmas. But true Advent waiting is much more unsettling than that. If there's waiting to be done here, it's Messiaen's kind of waiting, for the end of time itself, even if I'm not sure what that waiting means, nor how to do it.

One American theologian we interviewed said it meant living simultaneously in the knowledge that we might indeed be living in the last days, but equally we could be the forebears, the founders in whose wake a long, vast history would be built. To my surprise, I found it harder to imagine the 'founders' model than the 'last days' model. The idea that long millennia of advents stretch ahead of us seemed to cut against our widespread popular (even secular) apocalyptic beliefs. Surely something will finish us off within a couple of centuries? Climate change, nuclear conflagration, pandemic: delete as appropriate.

I keep having to remind myself that this flavour of 'apocalyptic' is far from Messiaen's 'end of time'. His vision is drawn to the other side of the cataclysm. Whatever brand of religious or secular Armageddon may deliver the end of the world, the *Quartet* begins where that ends. He believed that since the world was created by God he could draw on absolutely anything and everything in it to enrich his music. And he employs that radical creative freedom when writing of his longing for the end of time.

—

What does the angel say? The first copy of the Bible I owned was a small hardback of the Authorised King James Version. It was given to me in my teens as a birthday present by one of my friends, not as an aid to devotion but as a joke because of its cheesy illustrations – like stills from Hollywood biblical epics – and because it was a gift you didn't want to be seen with. Later, much later, it was the only one I had to hand when I started to question my beliefs and unbeliefs. In Revelation 10:6 in that version, the angel declares that 'there should be time no longer'. But in the Good News translation – of hotel bedside drawer fame – the same verse translates as 'There will be no more delay'. Most of the modern versions go with some variation on 'delay'. Messiaen was adamant that the correct version in French was *'Il n'y aura plus de Temps'*, though he was well aware of the different translations. Rebecca Rischin quotes him responding to the 'delay' translation with: 'That's not it. [It's] "there will be no more Time" with a capital "T".'

I can see why he dismissed it. Whichever way you translate from the Greek text, the angel is saying, 'This is it. Time's up. This world is coming to an end and you're about to meet your maker.' There are occasions when a *Quartet for the End of Delay* could be an anthem for me (late nights on Crewe Station platforms are up there). Messiaen made the right call. *End of Time* is the hook that gets people interested, as it did me years ago in that record shop, as it still does for many on concert listings. The idea that Time with a capital 'T' might end still gets my head spinning.

The end of time Messiaen longed for was the END OF TIME, the coming of a new heaven and a new earth, eternity. If you believe in that, then perhaps your own death is just a stop on the way to eternity. Time ends for you, then it ends. It sends me back to one of the strangest poems I know, Emily Dickinson's 'Because I could not stop for Death', with its deceptively insouciant first two lines: 'Because I could not stop for Death – / He kindly stopped for me –'. I like the impossibility of 'could not', the idea that stopping for death is not just being resisted, but declared impossible. It's the 'kindly' that has me snagging on it every time. Sometimes when I read it, 'kindly' seems naive, sometimes a sign of faith, sometimes almost sarcastic. The courtly, genteel ride in death's carriage that follows is no straightforward fulfilment of a longing. It gets colder, 'quivering and chill'; passing the stations of a life before concluding in the final stanza that 'the Horses' Heads / Were toward Eternity –'.

—

Nearly two months on. New Year's Eve. Mum has been with us for a few days. Last night, she went to bed before us, then came down an hour later, fully dressed. We were about to turn in. She said she had come back to show us a new dress, but she had been wearing it earlier. There have been a few of these moments. She is still quick-thinking, so she always comes up with a reason. Tonight, she is enjoying the noise and the company of children and grandchildren and their partners and friends. She and Dad always loved a shindig, often putting one on for the lull between Christmas and New Year. We switch the TV on to get the chimes. The Hogmanay show is coming to a close and I am dreading the moment they switch to Big Ben. When it comes, everyone raises a glass and I say 'To absent friends', which is the daftest thing to say about your father. So I add 'To Dad, who loved a party' and it's done. Absent friends sums up this night for me. Even when we were all still here, I looked forward to New Year's Eve after the post-Christmas lull, then hated the night itself.

Maybe that absence at its heart explains why New Year poems are often so full and noisy. I was reading Tennyson's 'Ring Out Wild Bells' for a radio adaptation of his epic dirge *In Memoriam A. H. H.*, written in response to the death of his beloved friend Arthur Hallam, and was reminded of another poet, Tennyson's wild mystic contemporary Francis Thompson. Thompson was a Lancastrian, born in Preston as I was, so I've always felt some geographical connection with him. His attempt at a New Year poem 'New Year's Chimes' reminds me why the connection isn't always that easy. It's a sweeping, breathless poem – not dissimilar in tone to his famous ode 'The Hound of Heaven', but like the Hound, it overbalances in places. Thompson was not a man for half measures – a visionary, an opium addict, a man who slept rough on the streets of London and was rescued by a woman driven into prostitution by poverty. He lived life on the edge and over it, and his poems reflect that. The sheer rush of the voice can be exhilarating, but it can be incomprehensible too, caught in the twists and turns of his personal theology and (in the case of 'New Year's Chimes') cosmology: 'From stellate peak to peak is tossed a voice of wonder, / And the height stoops down to the depths thereunder, / And sun leans forth to his brother-sun. / And the more ample years unfold / (With a million songs as song of one).'

When John Donne writes about the nativity – 'immensity cloistered in thy dear womb' – the vessel is strong enough to carry the weight. The profundity of the Christmas story allows the poet to reach as far as his language will let him. New Year doesn't have that strength, and there's nothing to bear the weight of cosmic significance in Thompson's poem. Perhaps the answer lies – as it often does in poetry – in zooming in, discovering the meaning in a detail.

I much prefer Thompson's beautiful short lyric 'To a Snowflake': 'What heart could have thought you? – /Past our devisal / (O filigree petal!) / Fashioned so purely, / Fragilely, surely, / From what Paradisal / Imagineless metal, / Too costly for cost? / Who hammered you, wrought you, / From argentine vapour?' He was a hard-working writer, even when homeless. To picture him – adrift on the mean streets of Victorian London – responding to a life-threatening blizzard by reaching for his notebook is amazing enough. But somehow Thompson managed to make a celebratory lyric, a poem of genuine wonder and minute observation, a midwinter poem worth remembering. Behind the detail of the snowflake lies the miracle of creation and re-creation.

—

What are years? Marianne Moore's is still one of the best – and toughest – questions raised in a poem. We know they come and go, but what shape are they? How do we mark them? I'm part of a generation – in England at least – who found our own landmarks through the year: school terms, football seasons, holidays, family anniversaries. We had a few shared staging posts: Christmas, Halloween, Easter (possibly), and a vague sense of progression through the four seasons.

But the journey of the liturgical calendar beginning – in western traditions – with Advent and working through Lent and ordinary time via weekly major and minor saints' days and feast days is so faint now as to be barely legible. Beneath it, fainter still, is the ghost pattern of a pagan year, often close in time and symbolism to the Christian. Growing up in a secular home, I had a passing awareness of feast days when they coincided with holidays, but there was one other landmark that stood out – Ash Wednesday, the first day of Lent. Nobody I knew marked the day in any way, but I liked the name. It was a day with a pull, an undertow. Whatever else was going on, it seemed to leave a mark on me. I have never kept a journal beyond the second week in January, but my notable Ash Wednesdays I find I can do from memory.

—

We nearly left Dad behind. In the crematorium car park a young man in a suit ran up to us with a paper carrier bag. I was reversing out of the space and nearly hit him. I got out and he handed me the urn. I told him we thought we were meant to pick it up later. We hadn't realised how soon – once the coffin went through the curtain – the urn would be ready to take home, I say. I nearly said we didn't know how long it took to gather them up behind the curtain. We put the bag in the footwell and drove to the wake. I tried not to think how it works. Did they shovel it into the urn like clearing out a grate at the end of the day? How did we know it was just him, not an amalgam of the ashes of everyone who slid through the curtain to the piped music that morning?

—

Last late snow of the winter, just as days are lengthening, as spring begins to drive the flower through the green fuse. We are in a Terrapin, a temporary classroom turned permanent, on the edge of a comprehensive school playing field in the mid-1970s. It is late afternoon, a race to see which end comes first, maths lesson, or teacher's tether.

Then the snow comes. Not much, just a few flakes outside the window, onto the field outside. The day is not cold, and the snow floats from a pure sky. No one expected it. The teacher abandons the lesson, and we rush outside to hold our hands up and catch the flakes.

Except it isn't snow at all. The clue was in the roar of jet engines before it came. This is a gift to us from the US Air Force. A nearby redundant airbase has just become active for the first time since the Second World War. It will become a jet fighter base, and these are the first of the F-111s arriving, flying low, shedding some kind of ash from the lining of their engines. Perhaps it is just one faulty engine. Whatever the cause, we will never see this again. Within a few years, the base will make another change, to host the 501st Tactical Missile Wing, and we will find ourselves living a mile down the road from Britain's largest arsenal of nuclear weapons. Then this chalk plain will become not just Greenham Common, but *Greenham Common*.

In spite of warnings from the teacher, we pick up the ash and watch it melt in our hands. The grey-blue flakes are more delicate than snow, ethereal even. They melt not because our hands are warm. They hold their own warmth. They vanish on our hands because they aren't meant to be here, and cannot survive contact with skin, or grass, or stone. We try to put some in our pockets, but when we check later our pockets are empty. How to mark it, this epiphany? For want of a ritual, I borrow one from a remembered school assembly. I take a jet-flake on my finger, then draw a cross on my forehead with it. This odd gesture has nothing to do with my secular upbringing. But I know it has something to do with solemnity, with power, with death. It is a serious thing to do. At least, I think I know those things.

The next day, rumours spread round school that the ash was radioactive, deliberately dropped to poison kids like us. I think I can feel a prickle of heat where the ash cross has marked me, as if I've been branded.

The ash that brands the brows in Ash Wednesday services is not just any ash. Its origin is a part of its liturgical power. On Palm Sunday, Christians celebrate the triumphal arrival of Jesus into Jerusalem. According to the gospels, word had got out about his teaching and prophecy and healing, and the people of the city lined the streets to welcome him, laying cut branches from the trees in his path to honour him. In an echo of this, today's worshippers are given crosses made from palm leaves. Now, for Ash Wednesday, the previous year's palm crosses are burnt, and their ashes are daubed on the foreheads of those same worshippers. The matter of Hosanna is turned into the matter of *You are dust, and to dust you shall return*.

The historian Eamon Duffy has written about the physicality of these symbols, reflecting on his Catholic childhood in Ireland: 'Its ritual absolutes and rules look legalistic, rubric-mad today; but they spoke with a sure confidence of the sacramentality of life, the rootedness of the sacred not in pious feelings or "spirituality", not in our heads or even exclusively in our hearts, but in the gritty and messy realities of life, birth and death, water and stone and fire, bread and wine.'

—

It is a long journey to Mount Carmel. We have satnav, but it's no use out here. This is the end of a two-week trip for our apocalyptic documentary series, and we have interviewed academics, preachers, even the well-groomed presenters of a cable news channel offering live coverage and analysis of the build-up to Armageddon. The visual style of their show is twenty-four-hour news – smart-suited presenters reading autocue – but the theological style is apocalyptic, based on the premise that we are living in the end times, and the clock is ticking. All of our real-world end-time events are examined in the light of the Book of Revelation as if it were a manual for contemporary global politics.

In a lecture theatre at Dallas Theological Seminary the day before, we heard the teacher assert that 'we employ a literalist hermeneutic'. What they mean is that the Book of Revelation isn't metaphor or myth. When it says that Christ will return at the end of the world, they mean a physical return. And we won't be waiting long. The end of the world is nigh, and some people know what it will look like. Now, in a sluggish hire car, the end times seem like a plausible idea. I don't employ a literalist hermeneutic when it comes to biblical texts about apocalypse, but this trip has got under my skin, and I think that if the end is going to come, then it might as well come here, on these remote Texan roads, where the world seems more than ready to receive it. We cast clouds of dried earth behind us as we pelt down straight tracks with occasional farms the only landmarks. Bleak doesn't do it justice. This is the wilderness. In the town, we were told to 'drive out on that road for twenty-five minutes, then ask somebody'. But there's nobody here to ask. Since we left town we've seen two men and a dog. We didn't stop, because we hadn't reached the end of the road yet. And besides, the dog was spoiling for a fight, pulling at its leash to chase the car. We keep driving. The road narrows. All is flat. There's no sign of a camber, let alone a mount. We wonder if we've been duped. We stop to ask directions of an elderly couple, heading towards town in a pickup truck. When we say where we want to go they look at each other, then back at us with contempt. What are we? Ghouls? Why would we fish around there? For a minute, I think they're going to wind the window up and drive off without telling us. 'You've come too far,' says the woman. 'Turn around, back four miles to the water tower. Take the track to the right.' We thank her, and we're pulling away, when we catch her shout: 'There's nothing there mind. Just a heap of ashes.'

    She speaks the truth. Ashes there are. Burnt-out shells of cars around a central compound, the charred foundations of a set of buildings. It is late afternoon. The light is low and reddening. The only sound is crickets. Alongside the ruins, a sign reads 'WELCOME TO THE WORLD'S MOST PERSECUTED CHURCH'. This is Mount Carmel, near Waco in Texas. Here, on 19 April 1993, seventy-six men, women and children belonging to a group called the Branch Davidians died in a fire at the end of a siege by agents of the federal government. The siege had already cost the lives of six Branch Davidians and four agents. They were expecting an apocalypse, and they got one. The name David Koresh has found a place on the list of infamous cult leaders. We are here in the late 1990s, and the place still looks and feels like the end came yesterday.

We are not alone. At the edge of the site, an old caravan is covered in placards, press cuttings, hand-copied verses from scripture. A woman steps out to talk to us. She says she is the ex-wife of a former Branch Davidian leader. Now she has made a small museum here. Her mission is to set the record straight, to convince the world that the government started the fire, to counter what she saw as the 'terrible slander' that the Branch Davidians burnt their own people. As she shows us round the ruins, a big 4x4 rolls up. This is a Branch Davidian pastor, with his wife and young kids sitting quietly in the car. He has come to lead a Bible study on the site. So we get talking. He looks about forty, short and stocky with a well-trimmed goatee beard and a flushed complexion. I could picture him propping up a bar and railing against the Dallas Cowboys' slump in form. But his language is peppered with prophetic words from the Bible. The Branch Davidians themselves are named in honour of the coming messianic king – the new David in the Book of Isaiah: 'There shall come forth a shoot from the stump of Jesse, and a branch shall grow out of his roots.'

He keeps warning us – biblically – that if we don't make the right choices a serpent will leap up and bite us. There's something about his repetition, and the little lurch he does each time he repeats it, that makes us think he's imagining this bite being specifically located – on the arse. Now I can't forget it. I'm losing his thread as he loops his way through prophecies and quotations and warnings, and all I can think is that he's warning us against being bitten on the arse. Iwan has caught this too. Next time he mentions the serpent, I have to swallow a laugh, but then I feel terrible about it, given where we are standing, given what happened here. Maybe I do need a warning, if that's the level of my complacency.

The Branch Davidians we meet here were not part of Koresh's group. But they speak the same language of prophecy and its fulfilment. They have scriptural texts that – they believe – predicted everything that happened here: the rise of Koresh's leadership, the separation from the rest of the movement, the confrontation, the siege, the deaths, the ashes. We've been here half an hour, and my colleague and I are edging our way back to the car. We've made some recordings for the radio, but now this is the last place on earth we want to linger. The pastor is giving us chapter and verse. It occurs to me that in his terms, he's not preaching at us, he's making sense of all this. In his way, he's explaining why this all ended in a heap of ashes. Not just why it did. But why it had to. There was no alternative. This was always going to happen, because it was written.

We are silent on our journey back to the airport. The

sun has almost gone, and we don't pass a single car or truck on our way. We talk about technicalities: the quality of the recording, the effects of the breeze on the microphone, the next day's schedule. I keep imagining us in the final shot of a film, a close-up of the speeding car pulling out wider and wider until we are too small to see, and the car is just a fast-moving shape, throwing up plumes of dust in its wake, lost in a vast flat wilderness.

—

'Because I do not hope to turn again / Because I do not hope / Because I do not hope to turn' . . . In his essay on Pascal, T. S. Eliot describes 'the demon of doubt which is inseparable from the spirit of belief'. His poem 'Ash Wednesday' – steeped in Dante's *Purgatorio* – is full of this duality. As a relatively recent convert, he has turned from the world to God, but is all too aware of the risk of turning back. He does not hope to turn again. But he might.

The symbolic power of Ash Wednesday, the liturgy, Eliot's poem, it all points towards opposites, polarities: God and the world, life and death, good and evil, the desert and the garden. Those words of commination 'You are dust, and to dust you shall return' come from the Book of Genesis. They are the last words spoken by God to Adam and Eve as they are thrown out of the Garden of Eden.

As Christians turn towards Lent, they are challenged to turn and walk into the desert. This is not just a way of marking the journey of Jesus into the wilderness, his confrontation with evil and temptation, his growing realisation of the path his life must take. It is also, for every believer, a journey into their own wilderness, a willingness to look into their own darkness. Penitence is essentially an act of turning, or re-turning. As Eliot has it: 'The desert in the garden the garden in the desert / Of drouth, spitting from the mouth the withered apple-seed.'

And what will our deserts be like? There's a question. I think of mine as dotted with tatty motels and gated holiday homes with endlessly watered strips of unnatural lawn. A pair of huge dogs sleep in the shade of a whitewashed garden wall under tree-high cacti. And somewhere out there is an abandoned spaghetti-western movie set, with saloon doors that swing and creak in the wind.

—

A hotel lounge at the airport. We are booked on a crack-of-dawn flight home, and still reeling from the Mount Carmel trip. A businessman walks in, sets down his briefcase on the bar and orders a bourbon. We are distracted by him, because he looks like he's been in a fight. He has a bruise on his forehead, as if someone headbutted him. He sees that we're watching him and gives a nod of acknowledgement. He's joined by a woman, also in business garb. We're within earshot, so we can't talk about them, but we both notice that she has a bruise on her brow too, even stronger and darker than his.

Remember, you are dust, and to dust you shall return.

Caught up in our schedule, and the stresses of recording, we forgot what day it was. Across the world, Christians lined up first thing this morning to have a cross daubed in ashes on their foreheads, a visible mark of belief and penitence, a mark of re-commitment and a way of saying: I do not hope to turn again. By this late stage of the day, those crosses are fading to a smudge, a home-made tattoo. And you cannot wash it off. You have to wait for it to wear off. You are meant to be seen with it, a visible mark or taint. If it provokes questions or comments, so be it. This is a form of witness, and a form of penance.

Remember, you are dust, and to dust you shall return. Those words, murmured as the priest dips a thumb in a bowl of ash and daubs your forehead, are about as strange as liturgical lines come. They seem anti-modern, even anti-human. How does this play in parts of the world where worshippers struggle against poverty, injustice and despair? And even in the opulent west, where our business couple sip their drinks in the airport hotel bar, what good can come of it? Tomorrow morning, they, like us, will browse the news stand in the departure lounge, and be tempted by the promise to Unleash the Tiger Within, or to learn What They Don't Teach You at Harvard Business School, or to Use NLP to Achieve your Career Potential.

But I'm thinking about the preacher we met at Mount Carmel. In his own way, he was writing *Paradise Lost*. It was the poet and critic Jeffrey Wainwright who showed me that Milton – writing at a time when the post-Civil War English republic was collapsing around him – was trying to explain how the world got the way it is. Its intention (stated by

Milton as 'to justify the ways of God to men') was practical and contemporary. How did we end up in this mess? To understand that, you have to go back to the beginning of the story, to the Garden of Eden, in Milton's view. And the preacher at Waco was trying to explain to us two bemused foreigners how his people ended up as a heap of ashes.

The smart couple in business garb sit down at a table next to us. They nod and smile to us politely. I wonder if they have forgotten the marks on their foreheads. But then the woman brushes her hair back from her brow, and the way she does it shows that she is guarding the mark, preserving it. Because for her, that cross is more than a reminder of mortality and a gesture of penance. It is an explanation of where we are, and how we got here. Remember, you are dust, and to dust you shall return. And it seems to me this could be the best antidote to what happened at Mount Carmel. This is deep-rooted, symbolically powerful religion. The way out of false apocalypticism – bad religion, if you like – is not a flight from religion. Secular faiths can be every bit as apocalyptic.

—

In Andrei Tarkovsky's film *The Sacrifice*, a retired actor (and atheist) called Alexander lives with his wife, teenage daughter and young son in a remote house on the Swedish coast. When the TV news warns of imminent nuclear Armageddon, he makes a desperate deal with a God he's never believed in, that he will give up everyone and everything he loves – notably his young son – on condition that the world is spared. He wakes up the next morning to find fate 'reset': no nuclear wipeout, no threat, no end of the world. But then he has to keep his half of the bargain.

In a film full of lingering, atmospheric shots, the most haunting to me are repeated top-shots tracking down a street littered with the debris of disaster: upturned chairs, smashed cars, strewn clothing, and people running full tilt, falling over each other to escape. This warning, this nightmare punctuates the film, reminding Alexander of the threat so narrowly averted, a threat still hanging.

Is this the role of Ash Wednesday in the pattern of the year? A reminder of mortality, a foreshadowing of what will come to all of us? I used to see it that way. Now I think it's the opposite. Dust. Ash. Body. A recalibration. A counterweight to extremes of belief and unbelief, a counterweight to violence and hubris, to the risk that we start to believe our own propaganda. If this is spirituality, then it's not the kind that comes as ether, perfume.

—

The German theologian Dietrich Bonhoeffer wrote about 'costly grace' and contrasted it with 'cheap grace'. Cheap grace changes nothing, he said, but true grace costs you your life. It is the pearl of great price, the one you sell everything to buy.

—

Late 1990s, Greenham Common. It is unseasonably warm, the first hint of winter loosening its grip. It is Ash Wednesday. We have come to visit my parents, and our two eldest sons are young and relentless. One is teething, and defaults to a low-level moan when not fully entertained, while his brother is at the apex of his 'climbing phase': banisters, chests of drawers, kitchen cupboards, anything with footholds. When he tries to scale the treacherous back of the TV set, we decide it's time to take them out for a game of football. Instead of a park, my dad suggests we head up to the airbase. The fence, he says, has been cut into sections and rolled up like hay bales.

When I was approaching adolescence, my family moved (with my dad's job) from the industrial north-west of England to the south, to what my parents thought was a quiet market town. But the peace was short-lived. As the later stages of the Cold War intensified, and east and west squared up to threaten each other with 'mutually assured destruction', cruise missiles came to town, nesting in grass-covered concrete silos like long barrows. Within months, groups of women had set up peace camps around the perimeter of the base, and Greenham Common became an international focus for the debate about nuclear deterrence and disarmament.

The story of those years – late 1970s and early 80s – has been told in journalistic terms from two sides: the USAF, and the peace women. But there was a third community, a group whose story wasn't told, but whose experience mirrored that of a whole generation – the locals. We drove past the base on our way to school, where nuclear terrors were a big part of the playground chatter. We told secrets and lies. Some said they saw the missiles being moved in the night, to secret sylvan launch sites for an imminent strike. Some said their sisters' USAF boyfriends had kissed them goodbye for the last time, because 'it's all about to start'. And the news was full of it too – the peace women cutting the wire fence and breaking in waving flags of defiance, before being arrested.

Worst of all was the pervasive sense of dread and horror that this instant apocalypse may visit us at any time, as we lay awake at night, breathless and frozen at the sound of a plane overhead. Was this the first Soviet missile on its final descent? A single, blinding flash, and all of Greenham, Berkshire, most of southern England would be gone. I vividly recall the night in the mid-1980s when the BBC showed an ultra-realistic drama *Threads*, written by Barry Hines, depicting the aftermath of nuclear attack on Sheffield. No one joked about that at school the next day. Everyone imagined it was our town.

Three decades on, I was playing football with my kids on the old runway. People are walking their dogs on this terrifying ground, some of which has turned into a 'new business park', complete with high-tech software start-ups. Gorse, toads and five types of berry have returned to the unkempt heathland, formerly crew-cut by mowers twice a week. Underground, the labyrinth of secret tunnels, control rooms and bunkers has been sealed off intact. The military architecture has been stripped away. At least, almost all of it has. Only the missile silos remain, covered in turf and ivy. They were built to withstand an all-out nuclear attack and are therefore impervious to assault by bulldozer or JCB. The cost of getting rid of them outweighs the benefits. The whole place looks to me as other-worldly as a moonscape, and I find myself feeling almost nostalgic for the old base, the abandoned garden. Bizarre indeed, to feel nostalgia for a place that haunted our childhoods. I've broken back into my Eden, but it's been ransacked.

On our way out, through one of the old gates, we see a caravan draped in a No More Hiroshimas banner. Next to it, a maroon estate car looks rusted shut. There is no sign of anyone, but there are hanging baskets either side of the caravan door, and they look tended. To one side, a section of the grass verge has been carved out and planted, with green shoots about to burst. Someone has stayed and has made their own garden here.

I think of my sons and pray that they will have the lucky break that most of my generation did. We were haunted by a latent terror, but our war was cold. There was no conscription. You are dust, and to dust you shall return. Or, as Marianne Moore puts it in her poem 'What Are Years': 'All are / naked, none is safe.'

The young German pastor Dietrich Bonhoeffer wrote a heartbreaking letter, under the title 'Thoughts on the Day of the Baptism of Dietrich Wilhelm Rudiger Bethge in May 1944 in Tegel Prison, Berlin'. Less than a year later, he was executed by the Nazis for his role in a failed plot to assassinate Adolf Hitler. In this letter to the first of a new generation of his family, Bonhoeffer expresses something of his growing sense that Christianity itself is entering a new stage, in need of a new response from the next generation:

> By the time you have grown up, the church's form will have changed greatly . . . It is not for us to prophesy the day (though the day will come) when men will once more be called so to utter the word of God that the world will be changed and renewed by it. It will be a new language, perhaps quite non-religious, but liberating and redeeming – as was Jesus' language; it will shock people and yet overcome them by its power.

—

What will it be like, this new language? Like a piece of televised political oratory (probably not), a social media thread (please, no), a sinewy Marianne Moore stanza or a song or a whisper or a litany? A cross of ashes is a place to start.

—

Messiaen said the Book of Revelation was his key source for the ideas and images in *Quartet*. But he didn't take soundings from all of it. He was not making the music of four horsemen, or plagues, or the wrath of God. He stressed, when asked about the piece, that he was trying to realise his own longing for the end of time, not to offer a musical commentary on Revelation, so he took from the book only what he needed. Although much of his focus was on chapter ten, when the angel calls time, he doesn't go beyond verse seven, so the *Quartet* has nothing of the strange and beautiful story of the little book that gets eaten, that tastes sweet in the mouth but bitter in the belly:

> And the voice which I heard from heaven spake unto me again, and said, Go and take the little book which is open in the hand of the angel which standeth upon the sea and upon the earth. And I went unto the angel, and said unto him, Give me the little book. And he said unto me, Take it, and eat it up; and it shall make thy belly bitter, but it shall be in thy mouth sweet as honey. And I took the little book out of the angel's hand, and ate it up; and it was in my mouth sweet as honey: and as soon as I had eaten it, my belly was bitter. And he said unto me, Thou must prophesy again before many peoples, and nations, and tongues, and kings.

—

Clearing out the house after they both had gone, in one of Mum's many barely marked notebooks and diaries and exercise books and sketchbooks was a book she kept by the bed. On the first page it said that when she couldn't sleep she had decided to try writing, instead of reading or just listening to the World Service. Four short pieces, each a riff on some condiment, some ingredient. A kind of memoir, mainly of her childhood in Salford. In one, titled 'Sugar', a run on how rare it was during the war years, for a child, to taste anything so sweet. The rich treat of honey or the few fruits on the market. She never told us she was writing, though she had always read. It was impossible to tell, from the notebook, if she started writing before or after Dad had gone. But as with many of her memories of childhood, there was a bittersweetness to these riffs.

—

Called up in September 1939, medical orderly Olivier Messiaen was taken to a French military camp outside Verdun, where he formed friendships with a cellist called Étienne Pasquier and a clarinettist called Henri Akoka. Both had a significant impact on the making of the *Quartet*, and both were to play it at the premiere, along with the composer, as prisoners of war in Görlitz, Silesia two years later. For now, the German advance had slowed and the new recruits in camp lay in wait for the next assault. During those in-between weeks of waiting, Pasquier – who was in charge of watch rotas for the camp – was able to grant Messiaen's request to take the dawn shifts so he could listen to, and learn from, the choir of birds at first light each day. If waiting implies limbo, then I can't imagine that of him. He was born believing, and born a musician. Even sentry duty was part of his work. And listening to birdsong was vital.

—

Hall Hill field is a climate crucible. If the town's streets are treacherous with ice, the field turns polar. In high summer it sweats and steams. One hour ago, this small town was dizzy with heat. Shops for miles around sold out of fans within ten minutes of restocking. If we had an air-conditioned cafe or pub we would all have gone there eking out a coffee sip by sip. One food shop and the Bangladeshi restaurant on the corner were the only air-con havens so we holed up there. There are jokes about us not being equipped for this in north-west England, how we complain when it rains and then complain when it doesn't. But now this unseasonal heatwave has been broken by a storm so powerful, rain so biblical, that nobody can step outside. Peering through the window, I see trees in Hall Hill being shaken leafless. A flap of tarpaulin left there has taken flight. A single bird – jackdaw or rook-sized, but too far away to be sure – is doing an aerial version of a moonwalk. Dogs are barking, warning their human packs that the world is out of kilter. We know. We did it. This is a dance of fury.

—

SING FOR THE ANGEL WHO ANNOUNCES THE END OF TIME

FROM AN OPEN FIELD

Some days it is not a piece of land,
but field as in a box on screen,
or place in which a force prevails.

Start with this hawthorn tree
which marks where field meets ditch,
fly-tipped and litter-garlanded,

then zoom out to allotments,
a half-tended garden of earthly delights,
where a feral parakeet

seduces its reflection
in the glass of a long-scrapped,
half-rotted shed

until night drops and the other,
its perfect lover, its complementary half
is swallowed by the darkening frame

and the cock laments all night
until by sun-up its lack has drawn
all the greens out of the hills

the mosses and pitches,
all the billboards selling getaways,
and left the drained world pallid,

the parakeet itself lurid, furious and lime,
all the force of spring used up
on one dance of misdirection.

CHAPTER 3

Abyss of the Birds

The avian ghost in 'Abyss of the Birds', the third movement in the *Quartet*, is that of a blackbird, haunting and haunted. Messiaen's notes on this section are relatively brief. The abyss is Time, he says, with its weary melancholia. The birds are the opposite of Time, radiant with light, they are stars, rainbows and songs of joy. This third section was the one that captivated me on first listening and still does. It's not much of an exaggeration to say that as a listener in my early twenties, 'Abîme des oiseaux' was the *Quartet*. I didn't seek it out in isolation, dropping the needle into the third blank ring on the LP. It needed the build-up and follow-up of the other movements. But it was the main attraction. I remember thinking it was almost worth learning the clarinet from scratch, to find out how it feels to be the blackbird charmer whose notes draw the song up out of the abyss. I ruled this out on the grounds that since this movement reputedly tests professional clarinettists to the limits of their breath control, it would take me decades before I could even attempt it, at which point I may not have much breath left. To utter, instead of last words, a cracked attempt at a blackbird in an abyss would be a sad finale.

It was the birdsong that struck me the first time I

listened to the *Quartet* in my student room. It dips in and out of the whole piece, as it interrupts the never-quite-silence as you walk through woods. At times, the four instruments echo human songs – laments or keenings, passages full of longing, slow builds of calm and rushes of joy. Then the clarinet will break ranks into a blackbird's trill, a run of avian grace notes, or the violin becomes a nightingale, all with the composer's direction to play '*comme un oiseau*'. The *Quartet* is full of it, on clarinet, on violin, on piano and cello, they ventriloquise the voices of birds. I had never heard this before. In fact, I had never heard birdsong, or at least not truly heard it.

What Messiaen believed about birds amounts to more than admiration of their songs, though he spoke of them as the greatest exponents and teachers of music. His Paris Conservatoire professor Paul Dukas reportedly told his composition students to go out and learn from the birds. Young Olivier needed no encouragement. He had been experimenting with transcription of birdsong since his teens, trying to tease out the intricate patterns of their music. But there was a faith imperative too. At the very least, birds were in a different category from the rest of us creatures. As musicologist Paul Griffiths put it, birds for Messiaen were 'like angels or resurrected souls, free in flight and at one with God'.

—

Just as Messiaen had found space for a few pocket scores in his backpack, Henri Akoka had found space for his clarinet in his. Like Étienne Pasquier the cellist, Akoka was a highly trained professional musician, and like Pasquier he was excited to be in the company of a noted young composer. Inspired by the dawn chorus at Verdun, and in response to Akoka's requests to give him something to play, Messiaen began work on a clarinet solo. Or rather, he co-wrote it with the blackbirds and nightingales of Verdun. 'Abîme des oiseaux'. 'Abyss of the Birds'. He had me at the title, before I dropped the needle in the groove.

—

The composer's preferred approach was to track down birds in the wild, to sit with a notebook and trap their songs on paper in situ. By the end of his career, Messiaen had created an archive of more than 200 notebooks of birdsong notation, his *'cahiers de notations des chants d'oiseaux'*, now held in Paris by the Bibliothèque Nationale de France. In his later years, as recording kit became more portable and reliable, he would record their songs, allowing him later to replay and slow them down for greater accuracy. Part of the paradisal quality of birdsong is its blistering tempo, rapid progressions and range of microtones which we, with our fallen faculties, cannot keep up with. To make it comprehensible to us, it needs to be slowed and brought down to our level.

To consolidate his notes made on location, Messiaen cross-referenced with vinyl pressings of birdsong, many of them commercially produced from pioneering field recordings – originally on wax cylinders – by Ludwig Koch.

To my shame, as a consumer and maker of sound recordings, I had never heard of this pioneer until I was reading about birdsong in an essay on the British Library's website, by musicologist Delphine Evans. The essay said that several birdsongs from Koch's recordings found their way into Messiaen's music. It also said that the British Library had a substantial archive of Koch's recordings, many now digitised and available to listeners in the reading rooms.

Within seconds of the first click, I was transported. Blackbird: north Wembley, 25 May 1957, evening. The finest, to me, of all the bird musicians. Every blackbird has its own garden or square within which to sing, and every blackbird makes its own subtly distinctive set of songs, different from the one next door. This particular bird in a London suburb one spring evening over sixty years ago gave a performance so entrancing I kept looping back to the start. One of Ludwig Koch's hallmarks as a recordist, as Delphine Evans points out, is his ability to produce a rich panorama of sound while keeping the bird centre stage. The sense of scale is panoramic. Behind the blackbird, a couple of streets away, two or three young children are talking and playing. A woman's heels click past. Streets beyond them, metal kegs are being rolled along a pavement to be lowered into some pub's cellar. Then out beyond all these streets, so far out it sounds like it could be standing in a farmyard in the Chilterns, a dog is barking for its tea.

It reminds me of Edward Thomas's poem about an unexpected stop at a sleepy branch-line station called Adlestrop in an epiphanic moment of listening: 'And for that minute a blackbird sang / Close by, and round him, mistier, / Farther and farther, all the birds / Of Oxfordshire and Gloucestershire'. Thomas's birds were placed in this scene by the poet, conflating and reshaping entries from different notebooks, as the critic Edna Longley has shown, piecing together its sources on different trains, different stops, hearing different sounds on separate occasions during 1914 and 1915. The brilliance of the poem casts Thomas as recordist of his blackbird and its soundscape, whereas in fact he's the composer. Like Messiaen in the *Quartet*, he reshapes and repurposes ideas and compositions into new work. Koch's gifts and experience inform multiple decisions about equipment, place, time, weather and direction, but once the recording begins, all walk-on parts are out of his control. Until a composer comes and lifts your bird out of north Wembley, placing it in France or Poland or paradise or an abyss.

—

I never listened to birdsong until lockdown when the world contracted to the size of a house and a small garden. We were fortunate and grateful to have those, and in particular to have a crab apple tree in the middle of the garden which grew tall, uncut for two years, and became the view from the upstairs room where I write. A friend who lost her husband in midlife was told that she would know her grief was easing when she heard birdsong again. For her, as someone who had always heard it, the return of that music in the middle of a city was a significant milestone in her bereavement. I've always remembered this because when she told me I wondered what milestones would be there for those who had never heard birdsong in the first place. I knew it was there, but never listened to it. It was part of the soundtrack, nothing more. I have two close friends who are lifelong birders. They go on trips to fill tiny arcane gaps in their knowledge. This ruled it out as a hobby for me. It would be the equivalent of meeting one of the composers I work with, and playing them a tune I'd written.

For this and many other reasons I am not going to become a birder, except in the context of my own back garden. I started to look up the birds that clustered in our crab apple tree during the pandemic's rewilding. The flocks that customarily overflew the town to land in Hall Hill field began to treat the silent, empty streets around it as their territory too. The tree would be peppered with goldfinches, starlings, bullfinches, greenfinches, chiff-chaffs, sparrows, tits, jackdaws, rooks, a sparrowhawk, a pied woodpecker. No hummingbirds, lyre birds, white-rumped shama, but having never really looked at them before, the uncut tree turned my upstairs window into an aviary. Looking at them soon became secondary, though, to listening to them. And trying to record the songs of one bird in particular.

—

I click my way down through the list of Koch's recordings. Blackbird: north Wembley again, 25 May 1957, the same evening. This time the distant streets are quieter. The bird sounds a touch melancholic. Maybe it's later and the silent hours are looming. Then a train. A steam train. At that moment, the scene in my head slams into reverse. In spite of the remarkable, crystal quality of the sound, this recording is an instant relic. I like those widely shared film clips – colourised, slowed-down, smoothed-out versions of early film tests – of a busy street in Amsterdam or a garden game in Paris. The work done pulls them out of the jerky monochrome cage where they've been kept for over a century. They walk like us, they laugh like us. But they don't look like we do. They are forever trapped in the props of their period drama, however much their faces look like ours, however much their walks and laughs are recalibrated to match ours. And our own home movies do it too. Clips of my parents, of me and my sister stuck in costumes, in rooms decked out for a TV drama set twenty, thirty, forty years ago. Film cannot escape the trappings of its time, but sound recordings can. A bird, children playing, unloading kegs, pedestrians' heels, all sound as if they are happening now, a live broadcast one wall away from the room where you sit at a screen with headphones. Until a steam train comes.

The poet and broadcaster Seán Street has written beautifully about radio, sound itself and the recording of sound. He argues that a sound recording wins every time over a piece of film, because 'when you are watching a piece of film, you are consciously an observer of it. There's an event going on there that you are outside of, you are looking in as through a window at it going on. Whereas with a sound recording, you become part of it.' A microphone hears, but doesn't listen. Listening demands attention. If your thoughts are elsewhere, you can walk around all day hearing everything but not listening to any of it. Seán carries a small handheld recorder everywhere instead of a camera, because it's a more effective way to remember. He made a recording in Paris twenty years ago, revisiting old haunts with his wife Jo. As they were walking through the busy streets, talking, he started to record, switching off eventually when they stepped into a metro carriage. Now, he says, whenever he plays that recording he can see it. Everything. 'The colour of the pony that went by, the red shop sign on the opposite side of the boulevard as we were waiting for the lights to change. I can see rain coming in and it's incredibly potent.'

—

I have no voicemail recordings of Mum in my sound files. Latterly, when Dad was alive, he always took the calls and made them. With hindsight, I guess it was part of him – or her – not wanting to give away the slips and loops that were appearing in Mum's conversation.

—

One more clip of the same north Wembley blackbird in 1957, this time a close-up, with a distant car. Then a file dated the previous day, of a chaffinch in a still suburban garden. Each file I open offers an immersive experience beyond any virtual reality. I've always thought the cliché 'the pictures are better on radio' has a chippy undertow, as if sound without pictures needs some special pleading. It smacks of wireless nostalgia. But when it comes to playing with time, making distant past feel like intimate present, the cliché – for me at least – is true. I've listened to these clips for hours, each one only two to four minutes long. I take the headphones off and pack my bag. The curators have called time.

I was right to feel embarrassed at my ignorance of Ludwig Koch and his work. His first recording, now lost, was made on an Edison Phonograph given to the young Ludwig by his father. He collected voices like autographs, including a falsetto Bismarck, Caruso singing in Italian and a wax cylinder of all the great Bayreuth singers of his day. He even made recordings of First World War battles. His earliest captured birdsong – believed to be the first bird recording ever made – came from a syrup-voiced caged white-rumped shama in 1889. Koch was born into a musical Jewish family and was himself an accomplished violinist and singer. His musical career was ended by the First World War, but his interest in sound, and sound recording, never left him.

In the late 1920s he developed a new series of educational gramophone records based on field recordings paired with books. He fled Nazi Germany for Britain in 1936 and later that year produced a text and sound book called *Songs of Wild Birds*. His recording career took off and by the start of the Second World War he was working for the BBC. He became a regular broadcaster, a national treasure, a much-loved eccentric with a passion for wildlife recordings and a gift for communicating that passion. His strong German accent in broadcasts (reportedly much softer in person) was once compared to 'an Englishman imitating a German talking broken English' and was parodied by Peter Sellers. His signature black beret features in every photograph of him working, however remote the location, but the most striking detail of those pictures is the complex and cumbersome field recording equipment he used. Scaling cliffs or mountains to record a rare bird's song meant carrying the contents of a recording studio on your back.

—

Around the time I first heard the *Quartet*, I was trying to write a poem about a bird trap. I had seen a reproduction of Bruegel's painting *Winter Landscape with Ice Skaters and Bird Trap* and was caught by the detail on one side of what looks like an old door propped on a stick in the snow like a ramp. A scattering of dark birds – cut-outs from the snow – stand on and around it, some more wary wait on branches in the foreground. The boldest – or most desperate – of them peck at seeds strewn in the shadow under the door. A long string, barely visible at first glance, runs from the prop between two stunted trees into a small window, where an unseen figure waits to spring the trap.

I was fascinated by the trapped birds' point of view, a sudden plunge into the abyss. As soon as I had that notion

I had left behind the workings of Bruegel's trap, designed to cosh and flatten rather than enclose. But as with the skaters on the ice, a bad choice or chance could bring a sudden end to time, at least to your life's portion of it. I still haven't written the poem, four decades on. Can't get it right yet. Bruegel's ability to conjure panoramic scenes both utterly alive and shadowed by death and damnation, the one inseparable from the other, is so compelling. I have sat and stared at them in books and in the Bruegel room at the Kunsthistorisches Museum in Vienna, where four long walls of these paintings left me wandering from scene to scene not wanting to miss a detail. I was in the city on the W. H. Auden trail, and I'd read that he spent hours in this room in his final years, when he was living in the nearby village of Kirchstetten. His most celebrated Bruegel poem – 'Musée des Beaux Arts' – lauds the 'old masters' for their truth-telling about the nature of suffering, the way a boy – Icarus – can fall from the sky to his death but that is a mere detail, two pale legs disappearing into the sea, while in the foreground a field is ploughed, a bored shepherd and his dog daydream, 'someone else is eating or opening a window or just walking dully along'. In time, the paintings tell us, we will all be cast as oblivious bystander and as sufferer.

—

In many of Auden's poems, especially the early love poems, the end of love is present even as its passion and glory are at their height. In the second line of one of his greatest love poems – 'Lullaby', often known by its opening line 'Lay your sleeping head, my love' – comes 'Human on my faithless arm'. Like beauty, love will be burnt away by 'Time and fevers', but for now it is everything.

—

I heard a bittern's boom. Or was it a corncrake's ratchet? I'm not sure. It was years ago, on the island of Iona. I was with Seán Street, making recordings for a radio series on the sites of early Celtic Christianity. It had taken two days to get to the island by car and several boats. But now we were walking the same paths trodden by St Columba a thousand years before. Our plans for the series were unravelling, but in an interesting way. We had set out to understand what was distinctive about those early faith communities in Ireland who took the sea route north to the Scottish islands, up the west coast then down the east to Lindisfarne in Northumbria, in each place leaving monasteries, communities, missionaries. One bookseller told us adding the word 'Celtic' to the title of a book in the 'mind body spirit' section means adding a nought to the sales figures. The Celtic tradition seemed to some to offer a different kind of medieval spirituality, more ecologically aware, more feminist, more creative, with its scrollwork manuscripts and singable blessings. But these saints died a millennium ago and didn't leave a systematic guide to their belief and practice. There would be no point, since they saw the end of time coming long before we appeared. That's the trouble with the end of time. It's late. And it's getting later and later.

The academics we interviewed said saints Columba, Aidan, Patrick and co. – from what has been pieced together about them – sounded pretty similar to other European Christians of their time, albeit every region had its own accent. By the time we interviewed a Scottish academic – an expert on ancient Celtic Christian history and language and a monk himself – we realised the game was up. As he reached for a bottle of Laphroaig to welcome us, he lifted a large box file from the same shelf with a handwritten label 'Celtic Bollocks'. But none of this dismantling took anything away from these remarkable people and the places where they settled. Iona, like Lindisfarne, felt like no ordinary place. These were more than scenic and historic sites. I couldn't describe it then, as an atheist and sceptic, and I can't do much better now. It didn't feel calm. It felt turbulent, disturbed and disturbing, but that was because it mattered. Despite its remoteness, Iona felt like a focal point.

I remember the sound of the phone ringing more clearly than the sound of the bird. It was a call from home on the evening of our first day there, to say Ruth had been taken into hospital and it looked like we were going to lose our second child. This would not be the first miscarriage. There had been one before our first son came, and one after. There would be more too, before our third son, though we didn't know it then. I wanted to come back, but I was too late for the ferry to Mull across the Sound of Iona. In the evening I walked out, alone, around the abbey and the nunnery and the stacks of ancient stones. Not knowing any prayers, I talked to the 'three-person'd God' John Donne had begged in a poem to 'Batter my heart', to the God who was honoured in this place. I talked to the centuries of ghosts who knew what they were doing when they prayed here, in the hope that their belief might make up for the want of mine. Before I left on this trip, we had talked about naming this child to honour our Welsh and Irish families, but now I was promising that if it could be saved we would name the child for a Celtic saint. As if the promise of a name might somehow get a saint on our child's side.

—

Earlier that day Seán and I had interviewed a member of the modern Iona Community, an ecumenical group who restored the medieval Benedictine abbey here and built a community in Glasgow to work with the poor and sick and unemployed. She had quoted its founder George MacLeod saying, in response to a moment of good fortune, 'if you think that's a coincidence I hope you have a dull life'. So far, this place had been far from dull. Even before the call from home I felt unmoored. We had been told about the chance of recording a rare bird. A bittern, I think it was. Or maybe a corncrake. I knew little about either, except that Chaucer dropped a bittern's call into his *Canterbury Tales*, but I knew they were both rare. If we go out to a particular field facing the sea, in late afternoon, and wait, we might catch it. So we went, and waited, and caught it. It was a corncrake. I remember now. Like a ratchet getting tighter and tighter. We never saw it. Nobody here does. You only hear the call. A local resident told us that people who came to stay on Iona were enchanted at first to hear the rare corncrake's rasp outside their window, then a few weeks later they were throwing bricks at it.

In all those books with 'Celtic' in the title, the term 'thin place' is used to describe the particularity of places like Iona. I can see why. It comes from a sense that here the veil between this world and the next is near transparent. I get the metaphor, but there's something insipid about it to me, a whiff of ether. That's not how this place felt to me. It felt like a dense place, the air thick with souls, prayers, presences. Not a thin one. Clare Mac Cumhaill and Rachael Wiseman's book *Metaphysical Animals* is an account of how four women – Iris Murdoch, Elizabeth Anscombe, Philippa Foot and Mary Midgley – overcame the sterility of twentieth-century philosophy, insisting that human beings were more than meat. In the preface they set out in vivid terms the changed world picture these philosophers engendered: 'a rich tapestry of interlocking patterns, studded with objects of metaphysical power, teeming with plant, animal and human life. And we, the human individuals whose lives help to create and sustain those patterns and objects, are seen afresh as the kind of animal whose essence it is to question, create and love.' On that island I imagined how the world must have looked to those early believers – the air an ocean of spirits – good and evil – where the sound of sacred bells could clear the demons like a disinfectant spray, where the world was full of threats, but fuller of signs and wonders. I've felt it again in a few places since, a world 'studded with metaphysical power'. Then it dissipates. No one ever talks about pilgrimages to thick places. There should be a guidebook, for those who can't take any more of the thin ones. I've never returned to Iona, but our middle son has the name of a Celtic saint and we are forever grateful.

—

I get in touch with Seán to check my memory of the trip. He knew it was a corncrake, not a bittern. He reminds me that the corncrake wasn't the only bird we encountered on our travels to early Christian Celtic sites. There was a blackbird too, albeit a mythic one. Glendalough in County Wicklow is one of Ireland's ancient sacred sites, where a monastery was founded by St Kevin in the sixth century. I recall our guide there trying to persuade us to shin down a notoriously dangerous cliff face to see 'Kevin's bed', the saint's reputed hermitage, cut into the cliff. 'Go to the place of your greatest fear, and there you will find your greatest strength,' he said. Yeah, well, my greatest fear is not falling off a cliff face, so if there's no chance of finding my greatest strength there I'd rather not plunge into a lake.

Seamus Heaney has a fine poem called 'St Kevin and the Blackbird', telling the story of Kevin praying with arms outstretched, when a blackbird lands in his open palm and nests there: 'Kevin feels the warm eggs, the small breast, the tucked / Neat head and claws and, finding himself linked / Into the network of eternal life, / Is moved to pity.' The stoical saint holds his arm steady until the birds are 'hatched and fledged and flown.' The second half of the poem is a meditation, inviting the reader to imagine how it would feel 'since the whole thing's imagined anyhow' – the pain, the self-forgetfulness, the prayers. When I imagine it, I can't help thinking of the songs, so close to the ear.

—

I met up with the clarinettist Kate Romano, who has played that solo part in the *Quatuor pour la fin du temps* many times. I was intrigued to know what it was like to be the conjurer, the conduit, for Messiaen's angelic bird as it transcended the abyss. What do you do, as a professional musician, when the direction from the composer seems – to my eye – more poetic and mystical than practical? But perhaps I'm wrong. 'A tempo marking is, of course, really helpful,' says Kate. Words like 'fury', 'birdsong', 'timeless', 'sadness' are useful for obvious reasons: they give the player an indication of what the composer had in mind and they often confirm what the musical notation is suggesting ('Yeah, it looks like a fury kind of thing . . . oh good, that's what he says').

But what about the more 'out there' notes to the players, and in particular the composer's prefatory paragraphs that I've always found, by turns, baffling, infuriating and gorgeous? Are those any use to a player? 'For me, it's not especially important that he wrote those words,' Kate tells me.

> My job is to do the best I can with this music. I don't have to feel what Messiaen felt in order to play something that might be perceived as sounding mystical. In fact, it's far better I don't feel it, then I can focus entirely on playing the music well. If I play it well (i.e. accurately, sensitively), it leaves listeners free to experience it in a way that means something to them; which might be mystical or might be something else. I'm certainly not playing it 'mystically' (whatever that might mean); my concerns are musical and technical ones. For example, maintaining an even tone over the break or keeping the pitch completely steady over a long note or finding an unexpected tone colour.

—

In lieu of mastering the clarinet, I tried to capture blackbird song. This was in the middle of lockdown, so I had plenty of time to attempt it. My audio bird trap wasn't sophisticated. No lure required. Every day from March through June the blackbird sang from the crab apple tree outside my study window with barely an interval. It wasn't just a passing blackbird. This was its garden. Blackbirds are territorial, and unlike many birds, individual blackbirds have their own repertoire, their own leitmotifs. Meeting our neighbours in their garden during lockdown, I couldn't help but think the blackbird in their garden – though impressive – was not quite so richly virtuosic as the one in ours. Only two things could make our blackbird swallow his song – a prowling cat which triggered a staccato alarm call, and me switching on a recorder. I persisted with my attempts to capture the sound of our blackbird, knowing that the combined metaphors of entrapment and ownership made me a sound recordist from the ark. Some contemporary recordists and sound artists challenge the image of a solo figure standing under trees with a microphone in hand, trying to capture a clear and authentic soundtrack. Why not, instead, allow your own presence to be part of the soundtrack, step out from behind the recorder and make yourself heard, give the lie to the unseen, unheard, objective recordist and fess up? Fortunately, I have embraced this trope in my own recordings by breathing so loudly that it's impossible to concentrate on the other speaker's words or the bird's song. Now, when trying to record our blackbird, I set up the microphone and back away to conduct my breathing elsewhere. But even then our dog subverts it. Or the cat. Or a delivery van.

—

I did catch it in the end. On a May afternoon with interruptions, but the song – florid and deep-throated – is in my files now.

—

ABYSS OF THE BIRDS

The year after lockdown we were on a family getaway to Lindisfarne, another island (this one tidal) with a reputation as a thick place. We had been before but never seen the north beaches dotted with dead seabirds like this – herring gulls and lesser black-backed, kittiwakes and Arctic terns were all on the roll call of bird flu losses. The first trip I made here, when the tide came in and the causeway closed for the night, I heard the sound of a hundred motorbikes sparking and revving for a race. Then I was told it was the grey seals hauled up on the sandbanks, and this was their nightly song. 'Why don't you just google it?' said a friend when I walked down to Cuthbert's beach late one evening to try to record it. But I keep trying to capture it and failing. It always sounds too distant, the foreground too dominant. It never sounds like it does when you're standing there. I need a better microphone. I'll try again this summer. I'll get it one day.

Scrolling down the multiple Ludwig Koch recordings in the British Library database I come to 'grey seals'. He's got them too. Not only that, but he has a close-up recording of a baby grey seal on the shore of a Welsh island coughing. The accompanying text tells me he spent weeks scouting, researching, travelling and finally shinning down a cliff with recording kit the size and weight of a grey seal on his back. As recordists go, I feel like a lightweight. As if Koch's seal recordings aren't intimidating enough for a dilettante sound recordist like me, the composer and sound recordist Chris Watson made a series of four tracks under the title 'In St Cuthbert's Time', to mark the return of the Anglo-Saxon masterpiece the Lindisfarne Gospels to the north-east of England in 2013, for an exhibition at Durham

Cathedral. Watson researched and recreated the seventh-century sonic environment on this remote tidal island through the seasons when Eadfrith, Bishop of Lindisfarne, was creating such astonishing beauty in ink on vellum. It's an immersive experience, season by season, St Cuthbert's beloved eider ducks plus cuckoos, cows, stags and seals, snipe and skylarks, plus of course the sea and the gales. It's not just the sound that compels, it's the premise: that for a great work of art like the Lindisfarne Gospels to be made, the conditions of its making are an essential creative element. Eadfrith was not working in an anechoic chamber. The world around him, the seasons, was the soundscape in which he was immersed as he worked. It's no surprise that the illustrated pages are so full of local birds.

—

Seán Street tells me that Koch's musical background, as an accomplished tenor, meant that as a recordist he was always keen to isolate the particular avian performer as much as possible: 'If you could get the bird into the studio, Koch would have been happy, but you can't. So he actually had a team of beaters to get rid of any other birds.'

—

Not the lightest room, this wood-panelled salon in the Bibliotheque Nationale, but on a dazzling October day in Paris, it

ABYSS OF THE BIRDS

should be bright enough to see the pages. For three decades I've had it in mind to arrange this encounter, but never actually got around to it. I've been to the market, near Notre Dame, where Messiaen noted down the songs of caged birds, and to the aviary at the zoo where he went in search of more exotic melodies. I've stood outside the building, near the Centre Pompidou, where his family lived, and heard an unseasonably glorious evensong from a blackbird in a small, shabby square one block away. But this is the reason I came. These are the *cahiers*, well over two hundred of them, documenting Messiaen's lifelong fascination with birdsong. At first sight, they remind me of the music exercise books we were given at school, to learn how to put the dots on the staves. I have seen the odd image of these pages before, but nothing to suggest the beauty of them now. Everything in pencil, sometimes rapid, light of touch, with the urgency of working *en plein air*, on other pages firmer, surer redrafts, birdsong slowed down and smoothed out to be playable by mere humans. His mark-making has the quality of an artist's hand, but what really captivates me is his vignettes: setting the scene, prose-poems in the music's margins recording the date and time, location, weather, quality of light, colours in the landscape. If Ludwig Koch wanted the pure song of a bird, Messiaen needed the full epiphany.

—

Messiaen's dawn birdsong at Verdun was described by his cellist friend Pasquier as 'deafening'. Even in spring it is not like that where I live. Was this disparity due to place or time? Is it the coming of the 'silent spring' Rachel Carson warned about? Are there fewer birds and quieter, cowed by our constant racket? Whenever she came to visit us, Mum would comment on the birdsong. I always put it down to the closeness of Hall Hill, plus our neighbour's elaborate back-garden citadel of bird feeders and the suitability of our moss-covered crab apple tree as a waiting room for next door's feeding stations. Mum rejoiced in the bird choir, though I barely noticed it then.

I was away on a residency in Germany (and briefly, Poland, but more of that later) from the end of May to the start of July and when I got back I couldn't hear the birds. I mean, there weren't any. The odd wood pigeon, but not much else. No sight or sound of the blackbird. Such was the silence, compared with the time before my trip, that I started to think the bird flu was spreading inland. Soon, every park and garden in the north-west would fall silent. I was told that a bird was found at the foot of the crab apple tree a few weeks back. They said it did look like a blackbird. But it was too mutilated for a flu victim. A cat got it maybe, or a fox from the field. Unless it died of flu and then the cat got the corpse.

A book had arrived, one I'd ordered months ago. It was a sixth impression from 1946 of Ludwig Koch and E. M. Nicholson's *Songs of Wild Birds*, originally sold with two double-sided gramophone records (now missing) as a comprehensive guide to British birdsong. The cover flyleaf is worn and torn, but the insides are intact, including at the front a pullout birdsong chart listing sixty-three birds across the top and twelve months down the side. A bold line means they're singing in season. A dotted line means they are limbering up or petering out. I look up the blackbird. It peters out in early July and doesn't limber up again until February. Maybe they're not all dead. I'm sure everyone else knew that blackbird song was seasonal, but I'd never taken any notice.

—

I learnt a lot from Koch's small book. The strongest line on the chart – unbroken save a brief dotted summer break – is the robin, which sings its fiercely territorial head off all year round.

—

Titles for poems usually come last for me. But occasionally they come first. As soon as I saw the title of the *Quartet*'s third section I knew I wanted to write a poem under it. 'Abyss of the Birds'. It was so full and so empty. What kind of poem would sit under it? I started thinking about Nietzsche's abyss, into which you can stare, but not if you don't like being stared at in return. Or the motorcycle 'wall of death' I remember from fairs and circus shows as a child, with the rider starting at the bottom then nudging the speed up and up, the tilt of the bike a little lower each loop as it creeps up what looks like the inside of a giant wooden barrel. That title was in an old notebook for thirty years, waiting for some words to live up to it, to rise to it.

In Jakob Böhme's visions, the primal condition of God before creation is described as the '*Ungrund*', often translated as 'abyss'. Earlier translations use the word 'byss'. If the void, the essence of emptiness is the abyss, then the byss must be its opposite, the essence of fullness, of being, the ground of all that is. I look it up. I have a gigantic old edition of the *Compact Oxford English Dictionary*. It is called 'compact' not because it's pocket-sized. It is the size and weight of a large briefcase. It is called compact because the entire text of the *OED* is printed in minute text in order to pack the whole language into a single volume. Unreadable with the naked eye, it comes with an accompanying magnifier, so if you can lift it onto a table with enough light, it is full of treasures. I find 'byss'. Böhme is cited there, as is an old reference to byss as a term for the ocean bed. In the biblical translations of Wycliffe and Tyndale it's a kind of fine linen. It's a verb too, meaning to sing or hum children to sleep.

—

ABYSS OF BIRDS

It begins in song, in fact in songs, such chaos
it's as if each dead bird is reborn to join
the same dawn chorus: all those shot, mauled,
window-blind, the roadkill, those whose
gist gave out in mid-migration, those whose

picking at the dry soil drew a blank, now caught
in one tremendous rinse and swoon of multiples
then down the song stoops circling and the tone
slides from tin to wood to stone it tips into
the vortex of its making, a sheer weight
of song too great to hold still and the birds
themselves are sucked in with it, corkscrew
curl of down, crop, tail and crest until it all
collapses into one dun thrush, a dusk yard,
cherry bough, a single note swells in its gullet.

—

When Mum lost Dad she started to lose time too. With hindsight, he was holding it in place for her, correcting her when she said it would soon be Christmas, instead of Easter, or that one of the grandsons had left university not school. He had, whether consciously or unconsciously to help her, reinforced their daily routines and rituals, guarded and kept their liturgies of making meals, the TV shows they followed, the point in each day when they walked to the local shops to buy a paper. They never spoke about it to us, except to joke that she was 'being a bit vague again'. When she lost him, she lost her grip on the recent, replacing it with the immediate and the distant.

—

Messiaen says the abyss is Time which holds us, despairing, in its shattering grasp. Birds are its opposite, embodying our longing for light, for the stars. I'm not sure what it means to have a desire for stars. They are, after all, just a powder-blast of ancient light. At least that's all they are by the time they get to us. And they are well on the way to being replaced by genomics. Where once our fates were in the stars, now they are in our genes. Keats, in 'Bright Star', lauds their constancy: 'would I were stedfast as thou art'. And that fixed sense of purpose, of guidance, the patterns and constellations they form, gives the stars the appearance of a map, a code, a message or a series of messages, a set of diagrams or texts that must tell us everything if we could only decode them.

In the course of making a film about genomics years ago, I went to the Sanger Centre in Cambridge where the team under Sir John Sulston was racing to complete the first full map of the human genome. As testament to their belief that the genome was our common human property and inheritance, I was told that the electronic ticker-tape of letters – A, C, T and G – scrolling steadily above the head of the centre's reception desk was live gene-mapping being fed directly from the lab computers onto the worldwide web and into the public domain. I remember thinking this felt like a pinnacle – humanity had reached peak science, peak self-knowledge, peak mapping, peak writing. When the genome was completed, a book of the entire text was given to the Wellcome Collection on the Euston Road in London. It's not a gripping read, but I couldn't stop turning the pages. Now, with the *Quartet* in my head, I can't help but think of that strange and beautiful story from Revelation of the book that gets eaten, the one that tastes sweet in the mouth but bitter in the belly.

Messiaen's expansive, spectacular later work *Des canyons aux étoiles* (*From the Canyons to the Stars*) was inspired by the colossal night skies and birdsong of Bryce Canyon in Utah. It is, potentially, the most Messiaenic of his pieces, set out on a cosmic canvas, featuring a theology of creation and an impressive range of conventional and obscure percussion instruments including thunder sheets, a wind machine, reco-reco – a Brazilian scraper – and a set of tiny cymbals called crotales. Oh, and a whip. It also conjures ancient rocks and synaesthetic colours, and for want of one more sound to evoke all of this there's an instrument invented by the composer specially for this piece. Originally called the geophone, it's become known as the ocean drum and has been picked up by other composers. It is, essentially, a large upturned drum filled with thousands of lead pellets. When swirled by an accomplished percussionist, it makes a sound described by some as the earth shifting, though to me it sounds more like an ondes martenot with a bad throat. Messiaen's wife, the pianist Yvonne Loriod, described the car journey back from the maker Messiaen commissioned to make the geophone, with the new instrument in the back of the car playing itself each time they turned a corner. The overall effect of this elaborate sound world in *Des canyons* is hallucinatory. It is one of the strangest orchestral pieces I know.

—

MASSACRE OF THE INNOCENTS

It was just a handful – five or six –
but they spread themselves around us,
hid behind trees, began a *sotto voce*
incantation made of nonsense:
jingoistic rhymes, unsolvable riddles,
misplaced bits of liturgy.

But rattling as it did off countless boughs
and branches, this whispered cacophony
convinced us that an army
choked the forest. We pictured cities
laid to ruin on the roads from here,
battalions of starving, shattered men.

So we dropped our picks and knives,
knelt down, begged them to spare us.
As they trussed us up, one of them said
his had been a lullaby, then put his lips
up to my ear and sang:
lu lay, lu lay, o little tiny child . . .

—

The story goes that in June 1940, Messiaen and three fellow soldiers (all musicians) were trying to flee the German advance at Verdun, when they were cornered by enemy troops. In an account recorded in Christopher Dingle's

The Life of Messiaen, the composer describes their capture: 'We were taken prisoner in a forest, by means of choirs of speaking voices. The Germans posted themselves at the four points of the compass, in small numbers, and rhythmically scanned certain words. The different sources of the sounds of these words multiplied, giving the illusion of a large troop. The chorus closed in a small circle on the Frenchmen, who believed themselves outnumbered.'

How else would this composer be captured than with a sound trick? Late in his career, travelling with Yvonne Loriod, to capture in his notebooks and her tape recordings the birdsongs he needed for his compositions, she would fool the chosen bird into a call-and-response by playing a recorded song from the same species.

—

Following their capture in the forest, the French soldiers were ordered on a shattering seventy-kilometre march to a holding camp as a prelude to their deportation to Germany. So it was that – exhausted and uncertain of their fate – the musicians undertook the first play-through of a piece later known as 'Abîme des oiseaux' in an open field near Nancy, with the composer presiding, the cellist (absent of cello) holding up the handwritten score, and Henri Akoka sight-reading. On playing this new solo for clarinet, he was struck by the challenge it set for the player, not least in its tempo. The composer wanted this music to be unearthly slow, at times pushing at the limit of what it is possible to play, demanding extraordinary breath control. Akoka was the first clarinettist – or violinist, cellist, pianist – to struggle with the demands of what became the *Quartet*. Standards of musicianship are far higher today. Kate Romano tells me it is not so tough to play, for a contemporary clarinettist, but she adds a big caveat about the first performance in the camp:

> It was cold – bloody cold. That means that the clarinet would have been flat and the pads would have been full of water. It's horrible playing a cold clarinet; nothing works properly, intonation is dire and the sound becomes pinched and thin (wood and reeds don't respond well to cold). Even when you are continually blowing warm air down it, in an unheated room, especially in winter, it will still be unlikely to reach concert pitch. And we know that Messiaen had what was basically a pub piano – a 'honky tonk'. Let's assume Messiaen tried to tune it; but it's still a pretty basic old piano in freezing temperatures. My feeling is that you would have heard harmonics from the out-of-tune strings – that's what gives pub pianos their unique sound. So . . . there are four musicians playing chamber music (not just Messiaen's own music – they played other chamber music – Messiaen had some scores with him) and even with the best will in the world, it can't have been in tune. Not in the way they would normally have played. The clarinet would be flat and the piano wouldn't be in tune with itself. Even if the strings were tuned down to the pitch of the clarinet, it would be unstable for everyone. I think they would have been fighting a losing battle.

Now I wonder what that does to your ears over a prolonged period? If four fine musicians play together every day, and every day they can't really play in tune (no professional musician would want to play out of tune), do you start to grow accustomed to a new sound? Do you start hearing things differently after a while and do your ears adjust to a 'new' type of tuning? Or do you hear 'through' the troublesome intonation to a future time where it would all be in tune? And with all this going on, Messiaen fills the *Quartet for the End of Time* with UNISON OCTAVES! For EVERYONE! It's a stark way of exposing whatever sound they were creating, and I wonder if he was enjoying the extraordinary timbre of four instruments trying to play in tune and not quite managing to do so? (It's not an unusual idea – other composers such as Ligeti, Grisey and Murail explored sound in this way.) His ears might have started to embrace the strange chromatography of harmonics coming from the four instruments. Or perhaps he was simply writing for the future when he knew performances wouldn't be given under such exceptional circumstances. I often think about that when I play the piece...

—

This solo clarinet in what became the *Quartet*'s third movement, 'Abîme des oiseaux', is in part giving voice to a blackbird's song. Or rather, a slowed-down blackbird's song. Birds are such miraculous musicians that their phrases and progressions are too rapid for the human ear and brain to unravel. The blackbird's song comes in fragments too, a phrase and a pause, phrase and pause, phrase and pause, as if it's listening for a response. So Messiaen slowed the songs down, and the aching, echoing emptiness of the clarinet's voice in the abyss makes perfect sense of that. As songbirds go, the blackbird is a rich, honeyed baritone. That clue, as well as genetic connections with other birds, plus the darkness of its plumage, has led to the theory that blackbirds originally came from the deepest, densest canopies of primeval forests. A low voice cuts better through thick leaves and branches. They have evolved 'out of the woods', but their song is still there.

I know how the blackbirds feel. The woods lie deep within us too. Since the famous trial in 1960, *Lady Chatterley's Lover* has become associated with one thing only – its depiction of illicit sex between Constance Reid and her gamekeeper Oliver Mellors, who lives alone in the woods surrounding their country pile. I may be missing the point here, but as good as D. H. Lawrence undoubtedly is at describing sexual passion, his scene-setting of the woods where they take place, the woods where all is possible, is among the strongest in the novel: 'Even above the hissing boom of the larchwood, that spread its bristling, leafless, wolfish darkness on the down-slope, she heard the tinkle as of tiny water-bells. This place was a little sinister, cold, damp. Yet the well must have been a drinking-place for hundreds of years.' We're not out of the woods yet. Lady Chatterley spends most of the book wanting to get out of the house and life that are stifling her and into the woods. Lawrence has Mellors, after a night of passion, being woken by the dawn chorus: 'Then he woke up and looked at the light. The curtains were drawn. He listened to the loud wild calling of blackbirds and thrushes in the wood. It would be a brilliant morning, about half past five, his hour for rising. He had slept so fast! It was such a new day.'

W. H. Auden's house, in the village of Kirchstetten in Austria, stands at the edge of the Vienna Woods, where flat fields clot and tangle into acres and acres of forest. Now there's a walkway through those woods, honouring the poet, but standing in what used to be his study, and looking out at the dense interlacing of trees and paths, it isn't hard to understand what drew him to live here, on the edge of it, half in the woods and half out. Like D. H. Lawrence, Auden associated the health of the woods with our health, the well-being of a people: 'A culture is no better than its woods.'

—

Even among trees I am a poor listener. When I walk in the Peak District woods that rise up to the east of our town, I try to practise the active listening Seán Street talks about. Perhaps I need to be recording it, with headphones on, a kind of mediated listening that forces my attention and breaks my train of thought? I am listening inwards when I should be listening outwards. I call to mind Jason Allen-Paisant's poem 'Listen', which enacts the kind of attention I need to learn: 'close eyes listening try / to name the songs that play / from small twigs and needles / falling to pods of acacia / try to be the parts of the forest / learn their names by breathing'. But if I'm thinking of a poem on a walk I am not really listening.

—

The fascination of Bruegel's bird trap for the poem I was trying to write was not being trapped, so much as sudden darkness. And the fact that in the darkness there was no way of measuring time. Nor of knowing when or if it ended. The draft poem I tried to write in my twenties ran with this, the bird emerged and time had leapt forward in its absence of attention, of participation in the world. But darkness can be underwhelming too. I remember seeing two solar eclipses, or partial eclipses, and although I knew why they were happening, and what was happening, I was a bit nonplussed by the incompleteness of the darkness. Maybe I was in the wrong place at the wrong time. Byron has a poem called 'Darkness' which goes a stage further, imagining a world in which both sun and moon are suddenly and utterly extinguished. From then on it's a race to the last man or men, an apocalyptic thought experiment. I find it his most striking work, a dystopian vision in which the benighted humans, craving warmth and light, end up tearing the world and each other apart:

> And they did live by watchfires—and the thrones,
> The palaces of crowned kings—the huts,
> The habitations of all things which dwell,
> Were burnt for beacons; cities were consum'd,
> And men were gather'd round their blazing homes
> To look once more into each other's face.

For the poet, this thought experiment was helped along by the summer of 1816, when a distant volcanic explosion blanketed most of Europe in darkness. At the time, the volcano (Mount Tambora in Indonesia) didn't get the blame. While some were looking for rational or scientific explanations, many across Europe saw it as an end-time, apocalyptic event, a punishment or judgement from the Book of Revelation being meted out upon a sinful world. Byron, in exile from an England he had scandalised, had fled to Lake Geneva with the Shelleys – where Mary wrote her first draft of *Frankenstein* – and he took those apocalyptic portents to heart. The abyss of birds (and mammals and plants and everything) is in Byron's poem too: 'The world was void, / The populous and the powerful was a lump, / Seasonless, herbless, treeless, manless, lifeless.'

—

In central Berlin, that summer before I returned to find all the birds in our garden had perished – or just stopped singing, as it turned out – I was sitting in a cafe garden in a courtyard between towering office blocks when a blackbird struck up its early evening song. It took me a while, tracking the song's source, to see it high up on a fire escape above the cover of the young tall birches planted to bring a glimpse of the natural to the workers at their office windows. I had no recorder but I put my phone on the table and hoped it would pick something up. Across the courtyard, a group arrived from work to celebrate a birthday. I thought they would drown out the song, but the four tall walls made this courtyard its own abyss, amplified a song far deeper than the one in the crab apple at home, a blackbird-mezzo like molasses, heavier than the air, that floated down and filled the space around me. A phrase, then a pause, then a phrase, then a pause, as if trying to explain something for which there are no words.

—

Berlin has a passion for the *Quartet*'s other bird too. In April and May, nightingales stop here fresh from wintering in Africa, settling in the parks and gardens to sing their travelogues, often accompanied by human singers, violinists, cellists, clarinettists. My time in the city was a month too late for them, but I wouldn't swap my sound file of the blackbird on the fire escape.

—

ABYSS OF THE BIRDS

EPISODICS

I.M. DSR

(i)
I am allowed upstairs into the
room one final time before
as a morning deluge
on your window
forms a rood screen
to keep outside from in
but not enough

(ii)
not you
this is not your face
sudden tipped
against the wing of your chair
as if in sleep
on the windowsill a joke-
book half-read
TV powered down
so because you always
kissed me on top of my head
I kiss the top of this now
not your true brow
but as present
as your missing from

(iii)
our world uncompassed
turns on this one chair
a spindle
none of us
our whole
your sleepless nightwatch

(iv)
these words cannot hold
or conjure you
I felt I should take
a photograph one last of you
since we would never
be in the same room again
but then knew
I should not

(v)
November glory
rain to snow to
ice-clear hours cut quick
hidden details
rendered visible
this is the first day
in eight decades that has not held
you in its palm I wished so
much that you were of
in

ABYSS OF THE BIRDS

(vi)
nineteen months on
seventy-six messages still
on voicemail because
I know the first one is
from you and cannot
work my way back along a
rosary of pointless calls
I can only wait
neither listen nor delete
until our house is empty
play it to the walls
your voice so loved
now feared
for what its sounding out
might do to us
record it let it tell us
there's no urgency
it's nothing
you will call us back anon
and none
of this is done or will get done

(vii)
June
a bead curtain at the back door
keeps flies out
photographs
home movies

QUARTET FOR THE END OF TIME

I have looked and
none of them still
holds you in it
your sudden vanishing
has emptied them
left us with facsimiles
but still we have your voice
in amber

(viii)
what to do
about this play-out
you and not you there
un-listened-to yet somehow heard
that day I gave you all
the words you gave to me
of love of thankfulness
then kissed your grey-
black stripe of hair
and knew you were
will be not there

(ix)
your remark once
that when
you reached the next place met
your dad in his good black suit
your mum stooped in her
green glass beads

ABYSS OF THE BIRDS

then your ancestors
welcoming along the row
until they spoke
a tongue you didn't know
you would embrace
you are not caught
by this
not here
this fallen elegy
that misses every mark

(x)
a blue paisley bathrobe
in your fitfulness
you used to doze
in front of rolling news
screen now blanked
your head
bowed on a tilt not cold
not wax the same warmth
as this room the morning in it
now rude sun
chance gone to say the things
I'm sure you know
I mean
not least of gratitude

(xi)
I hear you say again and again

as once you told me
inside I am
always twenty-one
all continuity
you held together by
on-being and ongoing
now breaking
into episodes
a cut thread so glass beads
roll out across the floor

(xii)
at night I hear them
scatter to the edges
of each room
in search of cracks knot-holes
gaps under skirting boards
they drop
to the next floor down
and roll
then fall to floors
this house does not possess
another and another
night on night
looking for true ground

(xiii)
three years on
the message light

ABYSS OF THE BIRDS

                    still blinks
            this is what outside contains
            mud like slip and hillside sinks
            water rattles through the drains
                    under scrub trees
                    hawthorn elder
                lies a badger's rotten pelt
                        alive with

                        (xiv)
            There is nothing I can tell you.

CHAPTER 4

Interlude

It's not quite the same as 'Interlude', but it's close. The *Quartet*'s fourth movement has a simple title – 'Intermède'. In French it is a rather archaic operatic term for a short one-act performance in the middle of a long evening's entertainment. But in a piece called *Quartet for the End of Time* it has a different role. Originally written as a standalone piece, in the camp, for his three fellow prisoner-musicians, it has a lighter heart, almost playful. At less than two minutes long, it is the shortest of the movements. The composer's notes mark it as 'scherzo', from the Italian for 'joke'. It still fits, of course. The *Quartet* is – despite the genesis of some of the sections at different times – complete and coherent. The birdsong is there. But it has a different spirit. There is, to me, a macabre and surreal touch to the 'Intermède', as if it might be the signature tune to a country house ghost story.

—

The elegy I made for Dad ended up under the title 'Episodics', in response to the loss of his story at the moment

INTERLUDE

he died. I still wish I had recorded him in his final years, going through his life decade by decade, pushing him for details so I could hold it (him) together when the string broke. Except I can imagine his shrugs and head shakes if I pushed him to describe his friendship group at the age of fourteen – who gives a stuff about any of this? The poem was also a nod to me being a self-diagnosed 'episodic'.

—

I had just turned forty when I came across an essay by the philosopher Galen Strawson called 'Against Narrativity'. I remember sitting by the heater in the kitchen at my parents-in-law's house on a post-Christmas visit. I had the *Times Literary Supplement* to read, as this was the only house I knew with no TV in it. I was brought up to believe that background TV was the soundtrack to life, the very fabric of 'indoors'. Here, when conversation flagged, people picked up books. It did flag and I was glad I'd brought the paper. I read about new novels, biographies, memoirs, but then here was this philosopher challenging the assumption that we all have a life story.

In the essay, Strawson questions the reality of the 'life is a journey' metaphor and is critical of some of its effects. For some people the sense of life as the living-through of an autobiography with you as its protagonist makes sense, but for others it bears little or no resemblance to the way they experience life and identity. For the purposes of his argument, Strawson labels believers in 'life as a narrative' as Diachronics and non-believers Episodics. Diachronics have a strong sense of personal identity in the past. Their memories of past events are clear and reimagined and retold (even if just to themselves) frequently. For Episodics, life is experienced less as an unfolding story, more as a series of separate experiences and episodes.

Episodics may be less likely to plan their career paths. Some may live intensely in the present, others may seem (by Diachronic standards) aimless in the way they live from day to day. One of the central differences between the two lies in ways of looking at the past. Strawson argues (from his perspective as 'relatively Episodic') that 'It's clear to me that events in my remoter past didn't happen to me. But what does this amount to? It certainly doesn't mean that I don't have any "autobiographical" memories of these past experiences, I do. And they are certainly the experiences of the human being that I am. It does not, however, follow from this that I experience them as having happened to me, or indeed that they did happen to me. They certainly do not present as things that happened to me, and I think I'm strictly, literally correct in thinking that they did not happen to me.'

To argue against the necessary continuity of self through history seems shocking. Cue the moral twist to Strawson's argument. The Diachronics have seized the moral high ground, to such an extent that the 'life is a narrative' metaphor is seen as more than purely descriptive. Surely, morality can only apply to a life lived with a conscious sense of personal development and continuity? He questions that assumption. Episodics can and do prove

INTERLUDE

themselves equally capable of sustaining relationships, behaving selflessly towards others and generally functioning just as well as their Diachronic brothers and sisters in every other aspect of ethical living. 'Against Narrativity' goes on to cite examples of writers from both sides of this psychological divide, some (he argues) driven to create narratives because of their lack of a sense of story in their own lives.

I tore that page out of the newspaper, put it in my pocket to read again later, stared out of the window. Here, in a small town in the Welsh borders, decades could pass and the view out onto Church Street wouldn't change at all. The past is not another country, it's an endless expanse of parallel universes. Not even that, my life is a string of beads, each holding a single scene replaying over and over, but the string is wearing thinner and thinner as more scenes are added. Or there is no string, just a giant jar of beads, translucent like those weird risen bodies in the visions of Jakob Böhme. Whatever the metaphors, this felt like a revelation. I am an Episodic.

—

A white-robed monk leads me into a modern wing of the monastery. 'There's a board here, which will tell us where you're staying,' he says. We enter a dark hallway. On the board is a column with gold letters listing the rooms. All are named after saints. To the right of each saint's name is a brass slot with a card recording the name of that room's guest. There must be twenty rooms, but there are only two cards in the slots, both handwritten in elegant script. My name is not one of them. 'You don't exist,' says the monk.

A bell rings. I follow him into the abbey, where I'm handed a sheet so I can follow the Latin plainsong. The sheet says this service is called 'None'. It is the middle of the coldest winter for four decades, and I am sitting in the oldest working monastery in Britain, deep in the Scottish Highlands, listening to the oldest music I'm ever likely to hear. It is early afternoon, but 'None' means the ninth hour since the start of the Benedictine day. I do a quick count back, to work out when I'll be getting up tomorrow. I count again, but it's still true.

From the moment my car door slammed across the valley. I was aware of silence here as tangible. Nothing moves in the Glen of the Black Burn. I walk down windowless corridors. Not a trace of anyone. The nave itself, candlelit and cavernous, is a trap to lure the quiet from the hills and hold it. Silence has become incarnate. By the time my name-card is written, the word 'None' has got a hold on me. None as in nothing. No one. I've only been here half an hour, but with the absence of people, the bare walls of the monastery and the mile upon mile of frozen white around me, I can see myself slipping through my fingers.

—

W. H. Auden wrote a sequence of poems called *Horae Canonicae*, exploring his own Christian beliefs, and following the structure of the monastic day. In his poem about None, there is a chilling section in which he takes us 'To dark chateaux where wind sobs / In the pine-trees and telephones ring, / Inviting trouble, to a room, / Lit by one weak bulb, where our Double sits / Writing and does not look up.'

I am taken to my study-bedroom. It is depressingly bare. I mean, I wasn't expecting a Jacuzzi and Sky Sports, but this is bare. The 'one weak bulb' is in a desk lamp. The desk is a simple table. There is a single bed with sheets and blankets tucked up hospital-style, plus a sink. Fire regs are stuck to the back of the door, plus a laminated sheet with mealtimes and emergency numbers. That's it. I have come to write about the life of the monks. Their work of prayer and silence. I'm going to be here for about a week, because I fear that's all I'll be able to take. But I'll probably tell people I came for two weeks. Or three. Or a couple of months. If you can only stand a week in your own silent company, that sounds like an admission of shallowness. As the poet John Berryman put it: 'Ever to confess you're bored / means you have no // Inner Resources', before concluding that he has 'no / inner resources, because I am heavy bored'.

This is years ago. It is the early noughties. All our technology was supposed to turn to stone a few years before when multiple zeros hit the cyber-clocks. Either that or bird flu. We somehow made it this far into the new millennium, but it doesn't feel any more secure. When I got this offer to spend time in a monastery, it felt like a good vantage point from which to survey the end times. And the writing gives me something to focus on. I lift up the table and shuffle it in front of the window. I think I'll need all the distractions I can get. Work is the best way I know to protect me from myself.

I do like the notion of a study-bedroom, a place where life and work are inseparable, where poems and beliefs can be wrestled with and worked through. I have a postcard at home of Vincenzo Catena's *St Jerome in his Study*, with the saint resting his head on a hand as he pores over a manuscript. My study here at Pluscarden is simpler than Jerome's. He has a sleeping lion, and a quail pecking at his slippers. And there is a large statue of the crucified Christ looking down on him, to keep him focused on the urgency of his task. Art historians have noted that Jerome's crucifix does not seem to be attached to the desk and may be a vision. My study here has a crucifix above the bed, but it's not a vision. I've touched it. Each time I come back from one of the services, I half expect to find my double sitting at the desk, more real than I am, writing, oblivious to my arrival. I imagine him wearing the white Benedictine habit of the Pluscarden monks.

This is my monastic cell. I peer through my window and outside, pheasants – vivid and exotic as peacocks against the snow – stalk the grounds in search of scraps. Beyond them, the woods are hunched in afternoon darkness, deep and still. It's snowing again. On my way here, I thought the big issue would be the presence or absence of God, not the presence or absence of me. I think of Auden's 'None' poem, and the shattering loneliness of that doppelgänger image. I wonder how long I would have to live a monk's life (chaste,

INTERLUDE

untouched, and locked into an endlessly repeated series of rituals) before my mind conjured visions? There are twin traditions to the doppelgänger myth. One suggests that he who meets his double soon meets his death. The other says a meeting with your double is a direct meeting with God. My double has yet to show.

—

Mum fell at home. She had a couple of weeks in hospital, then was sent to a rehabilitation unit to work on her mobility. One visit a week was all we were permitted – pre-booked, wearing masks, gowns, gloves. Between those weekly visits, we had phone calls. Again pre-booked. It was after the second move, to the rehab unit, that she met her double. She didn't talk about her, she talked as her. This double was in her early forties, half Mum's age. Otherwise identical. One Sunday afternoon, we got an unexpected call, on a mobile phone she had borrowed from the woman in the next bed. She told us that she needed rescue, had been kidnapped, was being held against her will in another part of the country. All this sotto voce, so as not to give the game away. She was unclear how to tell her captors from her fellow hostages. We talked her through the fall again, the break, the hospital, the mending process at the rehabilitation place, the fact that her kidnappers were nurses and fellow patients. She came back to herself then, but shell-shocked.

My weekly visit. I set off an hour early, to make

sure I didn't miss it. You have to book a half-hour slot and there's no flexibility outside that. Usual Covid precautions – temperature checks when you go in, full PPE at the ward, etc. They ushered me through into a day room with a TV blaring out the news to one elderly man in the corner. At the opposite side of the room, by a big picture window, was a table where they had set up two chairs for my appointment to see Mum. The first indication that it wasn't going to be straightforward was when the nurse – who had said she would be back in a minute with Mum in a wheelchair – came back to tell me Mum was refusing to move from bed as she felt warm there and didn't have the energy to get into the chair. So I was allowed to sit with her on the ward. They drew the curtains around us. It was quiet and I was masked and Mum's hearing isn't good, so it was a shouted conversation at times.

She looked tiny. Skin and bone. Lying on her pillows at an angle – presumably to ease pressure on her hip – that looked awkward, her head propped up on lots of pillows. She was lost in a drift of white sheets and pillow cases, twisted and stunned like a bird that's hit a window. Her body had become a pale, mottled ghost of itself. It was a shock. She recognised me, was very pleased to see me, but to start with she was sleepy and confused. She didn't know where she was, nor what was wrong with her. 'I don't know what to do with myself,' she said. Then 'Just shoot me.' But she said she wasn't in great pain (they had managed to get her to accept painkillers now) and she didn't seem anxious. Since last week's visit, she had visibly weakened. There was a yoghurt and spoon, a jug of water and a full glass on the trolley by her bed – both untouched. I asked her if I could help with them so she let me take the lid off the yoghurt 'for later'. I passed her the water but she wouldn't let me lift it to her mouth. She insisted on trying to give herself a drink, but lifting it to her lips was a great effort and I think she only got a sip. I tried again to help her, but she didn't want me to.

The conversation was strange in some ways – the pandemic was a real presence and she kept raising it, worrying whether we were all vaccinated, worrying she would give me the virus by touching my hand to take the glass. And she kept asking me to shush for a second and listen to how quiet it was, the world shut down by the pandemic, even though there was a road just outside. I had resolved on the drive over that I must say the things I never got to say to Dad because he died so suddenly. So I did. She said how proud of us all she is. I kept saying that she's here to get better so we can all come and see her once she's back in the world, but she didn't look like she believed it. Although her voice was weak she really looked at me. It sounds an odd thing to say, but her eyes were clear and loving and strong. There was still a lot of confusion, going round the houses about what all the grandsons are doing, but I felt it was a better conversation than last time. More real, more about the things that matter. When my half-hour was up, I told her I loved her and she said she loved me and all of us.

—

A day or two later we have our booked phone call. Today the rehabilitation unit has become, for her, a pub called the Rowbarge. She is there for lunch with a group of friends, she says. She breaks off and laughs at a joke. She is having a high old time. Their food is about to arrive, so she can't talk for long now, but she should be home in an hour or two and she will call us just as soon as she gets back to catch up on all our news.

—

As compline comes to an end each night, the monks kneel in front of a statue of Mary, to whom the abbey is dedicated. They look intense, moved, passionately involved in what they are doing. I am moved to watch them, to be transported by the music and the place, but it feels almost indecent to be gawping. One by one – as their devotions are finished – they walk out, heads bowed. This is the last office of the monastic day. It is quiet and dark, save the few tall candles on the altar. Frustratingly, from the side chapel I cannot see the statue that inspires such apparent reverie. My view is partially blocked by a vast wooden candle holder on the floor in front of me, taller than I am. Its base is ornately carved with what seem to be writhing naked classical figures. The evening plainsong is achingly beautiful, as the community gives thanks for another day, and prays for God's blessing and protection through the night. In a service like this one, it is possible to imagine a kind of rapture taking hold. Accounts of the ecstatic experience of God's presence have been part of western monastic writings for centuries, perhaps most famously described by Teresa of Ávila, a sixteenth-century Spanish nun, who experienced the heights of physical pleasure and agony during prayer. Is this the reward for celibacy?

These Benedictines don't see it that way. 'We're not here for spiritual kicks at all,' said Fr Benedict earlier, when I seized the chance for a question during a brief gap in his liturgical schedule. 'We are here for hope, and through that, we get glimpses of heaven.' He explained that he is 'rather allergic' to the idea of 'experiencing' God. 'It's making God into a kind of commodity, something that's there to satisfy my needs. But that's not it at all. It's so much bigger than that. God is way, way, way beyond anything else we could describe as "experience".' Fr Benedict is one of the older monks, approaching retirement age in the outside world. But in here there's no slowing down. Like the other monks, he is lean (no Friar Tucks, despite the hearty cooking) and vital. For some reason, I'd expected them to be lower in wattage, as if years of silence and prayer had dialled down their metabolisms, slowing them in readiness for death. But in my brief conversations when the silence lifts, I find them to be witty, engaged, astute and wryly aware of how they – and their lives – are perceived by outsiders like me.

I've always envied those whose faith manifests itself in direct experience of God. In a monastic community like this, divine revelation comes through silence. But over the years, I've been a witness once or twice when charismatic evangelicals got swept up into speaking in tongues. It has been described to me as a sudden change, a sense that you are not the one praying any more, but that God is praying in you, a fast and fluent song of joy and presence, a letting go. I'm enough of a sceptic to question it, and I've heard tales of fakery, of some half-willed gibberish presented as divine. I know what it means to long for such direct and intense religious experience, as a confirmation and a kind of transformation, but I fear it too. Perhaps for that reason, I'm still waiting. I think of Fr Benedict's reference to 'glimpses of heaven'. Here it feels possible. Or rather, if it doesn't happen here, I'm not sure where it would. Everything about this place – the remoteness, the simplicity, the routine, the silence – is designed to get as much of this world out of the way, in the hope of a sighting of the next one. It may feel more like the edge of the world than the end of it, but it's nothing if not apocalyptic.

—

My grandma had an old wooden dustpan with a matching curved brush, to sweep the crumbs off tables after formal meals. She had picked it up in a junk shop and never used it. There wasn't much need for it on her kitchen table in Salford. So when we visited, we kids would pretend to clear up after imaginary banquets. At Pluscarden there comes a moment after dinner when the monks pass these wooden dustpans down the table. As each one finishes, he passes the brush along, wipes knife and fork on his white napkin,

INTERLUDE

and stows them on a shelf beneath the table. Then he sits back and raises his hood. When all hoods are up, the meal is over.

The brush is not the only aspect of the meal that reminds me of childhood. Like most adults, I can barely remember what it feels like to be read to, but here at each meal a monk stands in a high stone pulpit to one side of the refectory and reads us a story. This tradition goes back centuries in Benedictine life, but now the books range from biographies to books on genetics or history. Tonight, it is a biography of the late Cardinal Winning of Glasgow. It tells the story of the controversial cardinal's battles with politicians and the media. At various points, in response to funny lines, the monks smile or laugh into their napkins. The monk who reads to us has an Australian accent. His voice is hesitant and rather flat. The whole experience is strangely comforting.

We sit evenly spaced along tables, and not one monk catches the eye of another. This at least enables me to indulge my habit of staring. It is like a meal for hermits, gathered in the same room. They carry the silence of their cells with them, even in these communal spaces. I like being read to, but the lack of response, the inability to thank the man who cooked your food, the impossibility of a brief word about the snow outside, feels like a lack. The food is simple but good, mostly home-grown vegetables and fruit. No one asks anyone else to pass the salt.

—

There is a common room in the guest house, with a table and six chairs. Above the table hangs a single, bright bulb. I've never seen that light switched off, nor the curtains drawn. It seems to burn round the clock, to offer a place of clarity, solidity, for guests who may feel the world is slipping away from them. By half past eight in the evening, the monks have retired to their cells. Tonight, despite the early starts, I cannot sleep so early, so I head for the common room. My two fellow guests are already there, sitting in the one bulb's pool of light. Talk is not small in this common room. Here, detached from the world, we talk about science and religion.

Raised in a secular home, I became a teenage atheist. I thought religion was such a pernicious delusion that I should try to do something about it. I switched my university application from English to philosophy and theology and switched my choice of college to an Oxford theological college full of ministerial students. My self-appointed job was to convert fellow students back to good sense. By the end of my degree, I had lost my atheism. This had nothing to do with studying theology, and everything to do with studying philosophy, which made me see my atheism as a faith system every bit as flaky as religion. In fact, compared with Christianity, my old atheism began to seem less and less likely to be true. Ever since then – although the dialogue between faith and doubt goes on – I've called myself a believer.

Now, late at night in the wilds of Scotland, with the owls outside screeching to each other across the valley, I wonder if my wrestling with God came about by accident or my will or divine design. How about that for an idea – a creator God who cuts the strings of creation, to risk giving those creatures a more radical freedom? But with this freedom comes a sense of loss and sickness. And – tonight at least – sitting in the common room beneath the bulb of enlightenment – I believe the monks here may have found a way to reconnect with the source of our 'sickness', our deepest longing.

One of my fellow guests is in his sixties, he says, but looks ten years older. The other is my age. They have been here before and have a particular demon to fight. 'I'm sorry about the fridge,' says the older man with a laugh. 'Alcoholics crave sugar.' I'm beginning to crave alcohol. I wish I had smuggled a bottle of whisky in with me, to counter the silence, to fill the hours, to put up a barrier between myself and my self.

I go back to my room and stare at the blank page on my desk. I have come here to write, and I am not writing. Not a word. Up from my desk to draw the curtains, I peer out of my window into the failing light and watch one of the black-robed novices walk across the garden, hooded, dimly lit from the spillover of the common room's light bulb. It could be a scene from last year, or last century. In fact, would it look any different 700 years ago? Give or take the artificial light, and the odd tree, and the glimpse of a Nike tick on his trainers, no. I wonder if the monks learn to recognise each other by their gait, their size and shape. What is he doing out there? Is he one of the gardeners in the community? I wonder if they garden in their robes. The hooded monks are so thoroughly covered by their white or black clothes that a brother here could meet his doppelgänger and fail to recognise him.

—

A page in my notebook, 10 April. I spent an hour on the phone to Mum talking about a seed merchant's shop in Manchester. This was weeks before her break and her slide from hospital to rehab unit to care home in those final weeks. An early start for a Saturday morning. Alarm at eight, so I could be up and ready to call Mum at 8.30 sharp. This was prearranged with her carers, because they like to change her bed every now and then, but she hasn't allowed them to do it for weeks. My sister had been trying, using multiple distraction techniques, but Mum is proud and still sharp. She keeps insisting that it's not necessary or that she'll do it herself. So they suggested I should call fifteen minutes after the carer arrives for her morning visit, then keep Mum talking for fifteen minutes, then they can change the bed.

So I called at 8.30 and we started talking. Once we got off the subject of lockdown and how everybody was, she went back to where her memory is sharpest. Her maternal grandad worked at a seed merchant's shop in the centre of Manchester. He kept a beautiful small garden at home, but it wasn't enough so he also rented two allotments in Stretford, which he kept as 'one for eating and one for looking' – veg and flowers. She had strong recollections of the shop where he worked – Yates's Seeds in Peter Street – with its baskets of bulbs and walls of wooden drawers with ladders up to them, brass handles and scoops so customers could buy as many seeds of as many kinds as they wanted. By the time we hung up the call we'd been talking for an hour.

—

At times this abbey feels like a film set – with its costume, ritual, music – and we, the guests, peering in from a side chapel, separated from the monks by a rope. At Mass each day, special effects are added by the swinging of a great metal censer. The heavy, perfumed smoke hangs at head height like a bank of fog and blurs the lines between us. For some Protestants the use of incense is a disturbing sight, a reminder of the roots of the Catholic Mass in a theology of sacrifice. Christianity is inescapably bound up with sacrifice: the daily self-sacrifice of these monks as they seek to live out this tough life, and the sacrifice of self implied by the idea of 'conversion', the challenge to be 'born again'.

When I knew I was coming to Pluscarden I got back in touch with an acquaintance I hadn't seen for a few years. He is a young man who went straight from university into a monastery, but left after a decade of monastic life. When I last saw him, he had just left the order, and was trying to rebuild his life. It was all too raw to talk about. Now he is willing to talk, but without being named. He told me something of the price of monastic life: 'I think part of the way to the kingdom for a monk is a profound reckoning with human aloneness – sometimes loneliness – where we face ourselves as fractured and incomplete. A monk is supposed to keep to his cell and do battle there.'

—

I go back to my room in the middle of the day and catch my reflection in the window. The light casts my face in stark relief, and I have become my grandfather. There are very few mirrors in the monastery, and without my knowing I have aged forty years in less than a week. The monks look young for their years, but my doppelgänger in the glass looks hunched and haggard. Maybe it's the shock of those 4 a.m. starts. Or maybe it's my own progressive detachment. Can silence have a physical impact?

I draw the curtains and lie down in the darkness. This silence is too great, too deafening. It feels like a pressure, like I'm sinking too deep and will need to decompress to rise out of it. At home there is always sound, always something. I like the idea that every time we think we have found silence, there is another layer of sound beneath, like stripping off layer after layer of paint and wallpaper trying to get to the bare wall. Except that there is no bare wall at home, nor anywhere I've been. It's all wallpaper and paint. If there is some sound here, some strain of deeper, richer unearthly music, behind the silence, I can't hear it. This is the bare wall.

When a monk called in a few days ago to see if I was settling in, my room looked like an electronics store: laptop, headphones, radio and a smartphone that couldn't get a signal. The monk was kind and said nothing about all this. But it made me feel like a lightweight, surrounded by my props. How could I confront the big void – myself – with all this kit around me? Tonight, my cell is cold and lonely, and the radio is company. I miss my wife and sons, and the phone has failed me again. Its single block of network coverage slipped through the gap in the window frame and vanished into the hills. But the radio works. At minimal volume I can make out a football game. I bathe in the tinny jabber of the commentary.

—

'What are days for?' asked Philip Larkin in his poem 'Days'. Well, surely not for getting up at 4 a.m. The air is freezing. The water hurts as you rinse your face. How can it call itself a liquid when it's colder than the ice outside? I look down into the sink, and my face shivers on the water's surface. My days at home don't start like this.

'Recalled from the shades to be a seeing being, / From absence to be on display, / Without a name or history I wake / Between my body and the day.' The longer I stay here, the more lines from Auden's *Horae Canonicae* come back to me, and the more they ring true. He associates these lines with 'prime', the first office of daylight, a service conducted when others are sitting in cars, trains, on metros as they make their way to work. When, on my first day here, the monk told me I didn't exist, I laughed. But as the days pass, the space between my life at home and here gets wider and wider.

'Without a name or history I wake / Between my body and the day', Auden was right. That is the chasm here, the tension. When everything that 'self' means in the world is called in question, all that remains is the space, the tension between your body and the day. The monks have no career structure, no property, and no change in the pattern of their lives from one decade to the next. I have all those things, but they mean nothing here. I think I'm losing myself. And of course, this is the point. You lose a sense of self in order to find God. 'Always let go,' Fr Benedict said to me, 'never cling on. John of the Cross is fierce about this, and we strive for it, a constant letting go, to come closer to God.'

—

Through the services and meals at Pluscarden I've been particularly fascinated by the novices. What have they left behind? What do they think about this new life, as they lie in silence at night? And what did their families and friends make of it? 'Vocation is a very powerful, irresistible force,' said Fr Benedict. 'You only really do this because you have to. And it does mean that you let down parents and girlfriends. Some of us are on the brink of marriage when we come here.' I ask about the two youngest novices at Pluscarden, both in their early twenties. One has just completed a PhD in philosophy, 'and now he's doing the laundry', says Fr Benedict. The other was in the navy, working on submarines. Both are, he says, doing very well. But before they get their white robes they must serve an apprenticeship of five and a half years minimum.

The abbot tells me that Pluscarden, having gone through its lean years, now receives on average fifty serious requests a year to join the community, and the majority of these requests comes from under-twenty-fives. I think about my own sons, and what I would do if one of them wanted to take up this life. I do believe that the constant prayer of these monastic communities is important. The late poet and theologian John O'Donohue said that the daily work of these engine-rooms of prayer on behalf of the rest of us is more vital than anything that goes on in the Pentagon or the UN. Sometimes I can believe that. I like to think that I would support my sons in testing their vocation and encourage them to follow it through if it is real. But in reality, I would probably be heartbroken.

—

Depending on your choice of translation, Messiaen's notes for the fourth movement, 'Intermède', describe it as 'more exterior' than the other movements, or 'more superficial'. He's not exactly selling it. Though musically and rhythmically of a piece with the rest of the *Quartet*, I think what the composer is suggesting is a break in the intensity. I would never single it out for a listen, but I've always appreciated it as a bridge between two otherwise irreconcilably different sections. 'Abyss of the Birds' and 'Praise to the Eternity of Jesus' are two of the 'singles' I return to again and again. How do you segue from the haunting numinosity of the 'Abîme' to the aching beauty of the 'Louange'? By offering your listeners a shot of something bracing, a sharpener between courses.

—

One monastic morning, my phone – dead for days – offers up a tiny, fragile signal. I wait until 7 a.m., and call home. They are getting ready for work and school. The signal is very faint. I don't want to raise my voice in the silence of the guest house. We establish that everyone is fine, then give up on the call. Having discovered – through the pattern of ritual, reflection and solitude – a measure of detachment, I find myself suddenly reminded of the cost of being here. If you want to become a monk at Pluscarden, you have to commit to stability (to remain within a single community for your whole monastic life), to poverty, to obedience, to celibacy.

The insistence of most religions (including Christianity) on self-denial as an engine of transformation has always troubled me. I'm sure this is real wisdom, but so much art and literature seems to push in the other direction, all those poems urging *carpe diem*: do it now, risk everything for more experience. But the hunger is never sated. I love Edward Thomas's line at the end of his poem 'The Glory' – 'I cannot bite the day to the core.'

INTERLUDE

I switch my phone off and sit at my bare wooden desk. I do believe that if I stripped back my life to this Benedictine day, this cell, there would be riches. But outside, the sun is cutting hard against the banked snow. The day is beautiful. The French philosopher Simone Weil (whose work has been a great influence on me) was known at the Sorbonne as 'The Red Virgin' because of her radical politics and her avoidance of any kind of physical contact. This was before she had any interest in 'religion', but it seemed to be part of her commitment to truth. It was an essential part of her quest for 'the other'. There can't be many phrases that link 1970s TV comedies with Latin monasticism, but 'the other' seems to do it. 'The other' as a euphemism for sex must be another 'other' than the theological term for the source (and destination) of religious longing. But both are in the same territory. Both refer to an attempt to break out of the prison of the self, to encounter something, someone, beyond your own subjectivity. And there are risks attached to both, of course, risks to the self in that 'letting go'.

—

One of my fellow guests – a Glaswegian in his sixties – sits in front of me at every service, twisted to press his back against the radiator, teeth clenched in pain. Every now and then, he traces his fingertips along a fissure in the ancient stone wall. He does this twice or three times in each service, and he stares at his fingers as he does. Is he losing concentration, distracted for a moment from the plainsong? Or is he reminding himself of the cold solid fabric of material? This is the world. This is what he stands to lose.

—

Losing isn't easy. Especially when the self is the subject of the loss. In 1938, broken by factory work and injured in the Spanish Civil War, Simone Weil went on retreat to the Benedictine abbey at Solesmes. Not for the first or last time, she was suffering with skull-crushing headaches. As an atheist and anarchist, she did not go there to meet God. She came to recuperate, and to enjoy the aesthetic beauty of the plainsong, for which Solesmes was famous. Sitting through the daily round of offices, Weil described an effort of will, to lose herself in the beauty of the music and the building, to transcend her pain. But when she managed to 'let go', she got more than she bargained for. In a letter to a friend, she later described 'a presence more personal, more certain and more real than that of a human being; it was inaccessible both to sense and to imagination, and it resembled the love that irradiates the tenderest smile of somebody one loves'.

—

Listening to the same liturgies a lifetime later and a thousand miles north, I find myself longing for something as clear and definitive as Simone's encounter. If this place is about God's presence, then it seems to me just as

INTERLUDE

much about my absence. The mystics often wrote about achieving a kind of transparency, so God could see the world through you, like a foretaste of Böhme's resurrection bodies. The trick is, to get the self out of the way. But the self is complex. Although this place is teaching me that I don't exist – at least not in the way I thought – there is still a self there, far from transparent, as solid as a stone wall.

—

This is the body. This is the moment when a round, white wafer of unleavened bread is placed on your tongue, and you swallow it. This is the most intense physical, incarnational moment of the Benedictine day. Entering the side chapel for Mass, each visitor can pick up a wafer from a silver plate by the door and place it in the chalice standing next to it. At this point, bread is bread. It means nothing. Twenty minutes later, it is Christ's body.

This has always fascinated me. When I was an atheist, this mysterious claim of physical transformation seemed to me both shocking and irresistible. For the monks, this is the centrepiece of their life, the moment they receive the body and blood of Christ in the form of bread and wine, and they look utterly radiant as they take it, almost in tears, some of them, overwhelmed by it. W. H. Auden wrote that: 'You need not see what someone is doing / to know if it is his vocation, / you have only to watch his eyes: / a cook mixing a sauce, a surgeon / making a primary incision, / a clerk completing a bill of lading, / wear the same rapt expression,

/ forgetting themselves in a function. / How beautiful it is, that eye-on-the-object look.'

    I place a wafer in the chalice and wait for the moment when the priest walks to the side chapel. Body. This is it. And as I swallow it I am shocked again at this religion I became a part of. I do believe in the real presence in the Eucharist, and I do believe it can be – even should be – transformative. But the physicality of it, the unwillingness (in Catholic doctrine at least) to stop at symbolism or remembrance, still strikes me as astonishing and scandalous.

—

I fall asleep in my cell on my last afternoon. I wake up with a jolt and cannot remember where I am. I get up quickly and open the window to hear the multiple chimes as Black Burn Glen gives way to thaw. I wonder what this routine, this lifelong all-encompassing ritual would do to me, if I lived here for years. I look out at the fields of white, and remember Louis MacNeice's breathtaking poem 'Snow', and his conviction that 'World is crazier and more of it than we think, / Incorrigibly plural.' Does the life of a monk reduce that to four grey stone walls and Latin chant? Do these Benedictines miss out on what MacNeice calls 'The drunkenness of things being various'?

    Every day, as we head down the narrow track from the guest house to our side chapel, the other guests and I have had to go back for shovels to clear our path. As the thaw accelerates, more great slabs of snow drop from the guest house roof and block the way. The more we clear it, the more seems to fall. I am powerfully drawn to this place and have deep admiration for those who live this life. But for me, the pull of 'things being various' is too strong. As soon as I try to clear my mind, to transcend the business of living my life, I'm confronted again by the 'incorrigibly plural' world. For me, the place to encounter 'the other' is out there, amid the 'drunkenness'.

—

Two of the monks head out to wave me off. One of them says how much he likes my coat. I tell him it's nothing special, picked up in a sale, but in truth he's right. It is a good coat. He says it again, and I wonder if I should give it to him. At the end of Larkin's 'Days', the question 'What are days for?' remains unanswered. But the need to answer it 'Brings the priest and the doctor / In their long coats / Running over the fields.' I can picture this monk in my long, black coat running over the thawing hills. It would suit him. But I do up the buttons and walk to my car.

As I drive out of the glen, away from Pluscarden, I can picture my double, sitting at the bare desk in his cell, studying the rule of St Benedict. The trouble with a retreat, is that it isn't always clear when you should stop retreating. I was shocked how quickly I felt detached from home, from my life and work. I turn the corner onto the Elgin road and a field of rooks rises, like a blizzard in reverse. Houses are appearing on the horizon. Low-lying fields display an intricate calligraphy, a record of hooves, claws and boots. The world is coming back. The *intermède* is over.

—

Intermède. A space outside, a turning aside. In the introduction to his epic poem recounting his experiences as a private in the First World War, David Jones said he had called it *In Parenthesis* because it was written 'in a kind of space between – I don't know between quite what – but as you turn aside to do something', concluding that 'our curious type of existence here is altogether in parenthesis'.

CHAPTER 5

Praise to the Eternity of Jesus

'Louange à l'Éternité de Jésus'. Praise, or a eulogy, for the eternity of Jesus. Messiaen says the subject of this movement is Jesus as the Word, his divine side rather than the human. It begins with an achingly gorgeous phrase on the cello, with the composer's note on the score to the player that it should be 'infinitely slow' (thanks very much for that, maestro, say the cellists) and it is alive with overwhelming love.

—

This movement, like several other sections of *Quartet*, had a past life. 'Louange à l'Éternité de Jésus' had strong roots in a piece written by the composer in 1937 as a commission by the city of Paris for the great international exhibition. In this form, it appeared under the title *Fête des belles eaux*, or *Festival of Beautiful Waters*, and was performed on the banks of the Seine accompanied by fireworks and waterspouts. The musical forces changed too – from the ondes martenot of the water music to the cello, violin, piano and clarinet of the *Quartet*.

The composer's stated inspiration for the 1937 premiere on the Seine was the promise of the water of everlasting life from John's gospel, which – as musicologist Anthony Pople points out – doesn't seem wildly at odds with its refashioning as a piece about eternity. Nonetheless, as Pople says, 'a number of commentators have expressed misgivings about the implications of Messiaen's transcription of this movement, along with the final movement of the *Quatuor*, from earlier compositions in which the music does not have the same verbal connotations'. It's as if the integrity of the *Quartet* only holds if he devised every note from scratch in the Görlitz labour camp while meditating on the end of time.

The realisation that four of the eight movements were not conceived as part of what we now know as the *Quartet* only made me love it more. Not only did he base two of the movements – five and eight – on earlier scores he had written in different contexts, but another – the fourth – was written as a standalone piece when Messiaen arrived at the camp before he began work on the *Quartet*. The sublime third movement was written for Henri Akoka in northern France the previous year. All eight sections were essential to and inseparable from each other and the finished *Quartet*, even more if four of them predated the conception of the piece. It's like the lines, titles, images in poets' notebooks that just will not fit a single draft or notion until weeks, months, years later when all of a sudden they will. The dots on Messiaen's staves, his notebooks and scores, knew all about the *Quartet* before he did.

—

It's sometimes presented as a ta-da revelation, to discover the source of a piece of art in a different context, drawn from the artist's back catalogue, calling into question the purity of inspiration with roots in a completely different context. Except it's based on a theory of creativity followed by no artist ever. My notebooks are full of earlier versions of titles, lines and images in previous iterations that I couldn't get right, then one day they find their place in a new poem. The same applies to every poet, musician, painter or filmmaker I know. One of the best-loved poems of the twentieth century – W. H. Auden's elegy 'Stop All the Clocks' (or 'Funeral Blues'), with its heartbreaking recitation in the film *Four Weddings and a Funeral* – began life as a satire on the death of a tyrant. No one cares. But there's a reason why this myth of pure making attaches to the *Quartet for the End of Time*, since the story of its genesis has become more famous than the music itself.

—

Late October 2021, another *intermède*. Locked down again. The start of the second or third wave. Maybe the fourth. I forget now. We woke up to find the world had vanished during the night. At least, the virtual world was gone. Online was offline. Like Eliot on Margate Sands, our devices could connect nothing with nothing. We still had the real world, sluggish and dank outside the windows, but like everyone else who didn't work in Downing Street, we weren't getting out much. A recorded message on the helpline confirmed that there was a major fault in our area and the engineers were on their way to the scene. But it might be twenty-four hours before they could fix it. So for a day and a night we were granted the gift of location.

Among the gifts associated with the saints, bilocation seems to me to be overrated and unintentionally comical. Saints in receipt of this gift could perform a miracle in Genoa and deliver a homily in Chartres not just on the same day, but at exactly the same time. Practical applications of this gift are easy to picture, and could help improve work/life balance. But in an age when we can appear on screens in multiple kitchens, sheds and offices around the world at the same time, bilocation isn't what it used to be. In fact, the rarer gift now is the one that comes with a broadband shutdown.

Virtual meetings ditched, emails unanswerable, I remembered I had downloaded a Chekhov play from the BBC to watch on a train journey, then never got round to it. The production of *Uncle Vanya* was itself a sign of the times, lauded at its London opening in early 2020, derailed by the pandemic and then filmed in an empty theatre. In the final scene, just before the closing speech of hope, I was struck by something I'd barely noticed before when I'd seen it in the theatre. After the desolation, the departures, saying what could never be unsaid, blame, recrimination, misplaced loves and misspent lives, Sonya and Vanya sit down and start working through the estate's accounts. All I had remembered of the play's final scenes was Sonya's great monologue, addressed to her uncle, of faith in a future of rest and joy beyond death. But now what made most sense to me was Vanya's solemn reckoning up of the accounts.

—

Just over three months before watching this scene, I was sitting on one side of a hospital bed with my sister on the other side and our mum in between us. The call had come around midnight, and now we were well into the small hours.

All I had been told was that Mum had been taken from the care home where she had been recovering from a broken hip, and was now in hospital. My sister lived nearby and had been there when the ambulance arrived at the care home. When she called me, telling me to get in the car right now and put my foot down, nothing else needed to be said. There was only the odd car or truck to pass on the two-hour drive west. Small hours of Monday morning. Barely anyone about. I kept trying to think through what needed to be thought through at a time like this. What should I say to Mum if this was the last night? She had looked so frail the previous week when I saw her that I had said some of those things then – about love received and given, about gratitude, about her generosity and joy as a mother and grandmother. On my way home then I had seen a car bumper sticker with a Bible verse that seemed to confirm that it had been our final meeting. I don't remember what verse it was, only the conviction that such 'magical thinking' – as Joan Didion put it – was part of the fabric of grief, even when that grief had not yet come to pass.

    All you can do, I thought, when you have said your last things too soon, is to say them all again. In any case, repetition means something different now. For the past year, it's been clear that by the time we get from her care home room to the car park, she has forgotten we were ever there. Her own history, her stories, have become crystal liturgies, performed in conversation over and over again, word for word, inflection for inflection. There are no new ones. Her memory won't let her make any more. When we visited in recent weeks, she didn't know why the nurses made us put on masks, gloves, plastic smocks to sit by her bed. In her head, time has been slipping out of kilter for months now. We bought her a clock with a big digital display, but she forgets what it says as soon as she looks away. She told us, earlier in the summer when she was still at home, that the people on her road were a miserable bunch since she was the only one who went outside to clap for the NHS. Then she added that it was dark so she might not have seen them. Since it was summer and still full daylight at 8 p.m., we pictured Mum out there at 3 a.m., banging a pan with a spoon and waking up the neighbours. A year earlier, even six months, it's the kind of story she would find hysterical.

—

PRAISE TO THE ETERNITY OF JESUS

I can't think. I am just following the satnav. I know the way, but I set the route so I wouldn't get it wrong. There is so much to think about, I cannot keep my mind on how to get there. My head is full of bees. Instead of rehearsing my last words again, preparing for what I might see, coming to terms, I find myself counting. It takes a while to realise I am doing it – counting parked cars, counting trees and turnings, counting the number of upstairs rooms with lights still on in the small hours. In the garden of a bungalow before the hospital a row of shabby topiary animals has been given a topical twist with facemasks over the snouts. I count them too.

As soon as I give my name in A&E, I am rushed through a side door then led down dim-lit corridors at a jog. She has been moved to a room off the ward. A nurse stops me at the door and asks if I am okay, if I am ready, if I have prepared myself. When I ask how she is, how close it is, he said, 'Her bloods are deranged. She's only on oxygen as a kindness.' I asked if we were talking about a matter of hours. He said, 'Not even hours, there's no coming back from this.' My sister has nothing more to say. She has said it all already, while I was on those empty roads. She steps outside the room so I can say my lines. I say them quickly but I don't know what they mean. The nurse looks in. I ask him if Mum can hear me, and he says I should talk as if she can. Her eyes are open and at first I think she moves them to look at me, but then I notice they are moving slowly from left to right and back again, over and over in the same rhythm. I stare up at the ceiling where she is looking and I count all the ceiling tiles – twelve by eight. From what I can see, her world has contracted to a strip of four tiles from left to right, left to right, left to right with a tile-sized light at each end of the row. We sit for an hour or so, with occasional visits from the nurses. We talk to each other about Mum, to her directly, sit in silence some of the time, say prayers, stroke her forehead and hair, try to comfort her and reassure her. Her eyes are still scanning the row of tiles left to right and back.

Dad had gone suddenly. In the night. When I got to the house he was there, but absolutely not there. I never saw him cross the line, but there was no question that he was no longer there. No doubt at all. Now, with Mum, on a summer night in a hospital side room, the line between life and death is so faint as to be invisible. At first she was reaching, pulling for breath from the mask. Now the pattern of her breath grows fainter and fainter, until there is no pattern at all. Has she gone? We call in the nurse, who finds a vestigial pulse. It's barely there. But it's there. I thought these moments were meant to be clear, like in films when there is a discernible last sigh or a stillness falls across the face. But now it is impossible to tell if she is halfway down a corridor between one world and the next, if she can still hear our voices coming from some vanishing point behind her.

—

Chekhov's Sonya has things to say at the end of the play. Big, important things about days, disappointments, the necessity of carrying on. But Vanya – sitting at the table where estate accounts are filled in, sums tallied, books balanced – can only speak of rubles and kopeks. The words he has left at this late stage of a play where everything has been said – for better and for worse – are the names and figures on the invoices.

For weeks, months after that summer night, I was counting the kopeks. None of this is unusual. None of this is individual. It feels like a deep instinct. Phrases come to mind about putting your affairs in order. In William Carlos Williams's late, flawed, unfinished masterpiece of a poem *Paterson*, he includes an inventory of the belongings of one Cornelius Doremus, who died near Montville, New Jersey in 1803, including five sheets, eight caps, four pairs of breeches, two pocketbooks . . . all with a precise value in dollars and cents. The financial summation of a life is a political document, and its placing in *Paterson* was a political act. It was also a legal act, a reckoning up. Like Uncle Vanya and his niece on Professor Serebryakov's estate who had to keep on living and turned to numbers to achieve it. In Mum's case, there was a house to sort out, a house that had – in one night – changed from a place where she lived, where they both had lived, into a museum of their (and our) lives. They were of that post-war generation that kept everything 'just in case', so every cupboard was stuffed, every drawer. Dad had become, in his retirement, a reckoner-up, a list-maker, a keeper of inventories. After he died, we found a file called 'when we go' in which he had written lists of who to contact, what to do. Paper labels had been tied to all the keys saying which doors they opened. His own personal effects were labelled too, including nudges to assist us with a future clearance – 'cheap sunglasses – not worth keeping' – books full of handwritten tallies including one listing the contents of each kitchen cupboard.

After Dad's death, Mum went in the opposite direction. All her clothes came out of the wardrobe and were piled up on Dad's side of the bed. We tried clearing them up for her, but the heap would reappear shortly after each attempt. We wondered if she wanted the weight of the clothes, their bulk, in preference to a flat emptiness beside her when she woke in the night. Paperwork she had previously piled on a table now took over the floor in what looked like an unlit bonfire, and there was no inventory, no system. We would find, as we cleared a room, that any given pile of papers could include junk mail, half-finished drawings, torn-out newspaper stories, medical letters, an old photograph of her grandparents or a relic from their lives – her father's passport or exam certificate courtesy of the Salford School Board. We found a stash of letters written to her by Dad, her then fiancé, when he was on a stag trip to Scotland with his friends and writing back to her about the wedding plans. Should we read these? She had kept them, but when he wrote them there was clearly no intent for us – or anyone else – to see them.

I am capable of both my parents' modi operandi when their worlds shook. There is an inventory keeper in me for sure, a cataloguer, a man who makes field recordings of sounds he could easily find online, sorts them into folders and never listens back. But I get the pull of chaos too:

the strewn papers, heaps of clothes, as if a rigid tidiness somehow prefigured death, like putting your affairs in order.

—

By 1 a.m. or shortly after, her eye movements have steadied and she is looking straight upwards. After a while we call in the nurse. Although we never knew nor marked the moment, it must have passed because the pulse is traceless now. We both kiss her brow, then the nurse comes back and says he can't 'officially' declare her deceased, but a doctor would be along shortly to do that. He can't find any ghost of a heartbeat, nor any response to a torch shone into her eyes. This is about 1.30 a.m. The nurse asks us if Mum is wearing any rings. My sister says yes. He asks if we want to take them home and we say we will. He asks if my sister wants to remove the rings herself, but she shakes her head. It feels too soon. The nurse takes Mum's hand, but the rings are tight and need a twist and pull to get them off. He whispers 'Sorry, Iris, I'm sorry,' as the last one comes free. Then he leaves us alone, awaiting the doctor. For a while, even after the rings are gone, we are not certain. She still feels present somehow. We wait until it's clear that Mum is not there any more. Her face, stripped back and pale, has settled into a mask of her dad's face. Her mouth and eyes are open. We sit for ten minutes or so but it seems disrespectful, to look at her lifeless and set like that.

We move to a visitors' room with a few chairs and a low table. Our nurse returns and tells us the doctor has confirmed her death, and he is very sorry for our loss. He talks about next steps, funeral directors and sources of support if we needed them. Then he breaks down and sobs. He has only met Mum this evening, never well enough to have a conversation, but here he is in floods. My sister, sitting next to him, reaches across to put an arm around his shoulders. It has all been too much, the last year, the masks, the cordoned-off wards, the patients unable to draw enough breath. He looks utterly shattered and spent.

We are walked to the main exit and as we hit the open air and take our face masks off, I can hear a woman screaming in the opposite building, with a sign above the door saying 'Women and Children's Unit' and she is clearly a mother in labour.

—

I get home at about 3.30 and the boys are all in bed. The dog gave me a quiet but enthusiastic welcome back. Ruth is waiting up, so we sit at the kitchen table for an hour or so, raising glasses – to Mum – of the malt whisky the boys bought me for Father's Day, and talking about her, celebrating who she was, how much she loved us all and was loved in return. We went to bed just as the dawn chorus was starting up.

—

Vanya and Sonya are not the only characters in Chekhov's run-down rural estate to find themselves responding to age and accidie by keeping a record. At the same table where they were counting the kopeks, Dr Astrov had earlier been working on his maps. Unlike the accounts, the doctor's maps had no practical purpose. They functioned as a record of the decline of the forests. The decline was irreversible. His maps depict the landscape fifty years ago, then twenty-five, then now and with each iteration there is less green, fewer habitations, fewer elk, goats, swans and geese. But the maps are painstakingly made, things of beauty, precious enough to be rolled and never folded.

My mum's mapping in the last few years before her memory started to fail – perhaps because her memory was starting to fail – was a tracery of threads, tying people to places and ultimately, tying herself and us into a pattern she could draw up, a retrospective route map showing us how our genes drove us from the late eighteenth century to us and our children. It is an ancestral route map with lots of dead ends. I always had the feeling she was hoping for someone or something exceptional to turn up, some figure from the past who would light up the family tree, give us a sense of purpose, a story to tell about ourselves. So she started to map us online. On Dad's side, they were mainly Welsh publicans or drinkers, with a few Nonconformist ministers and schoolteachers thrown in. On Mum's side, the lines came from Greystones in County Wicklow to Salford and Manchester. They were millworkers, dockworkers, gardeners, merchant seafarers, a seed merchant, a phrenologist with a practice in Liverpool, but nobody she had heard of.

—

I didn't think much about Galen Strawson's essay 'Against Narrativity' in the years since I read it. That's the trouble with us Episodics, we can experience a life-defining epiphany then fail to follow it up because it happened to somebody else. But as I was trying to write about the loss of my dad it came back. The poem I had spent three years trying to finish had broken into different snapshots. They were poem-Polaroids taken at different times both before and after the morning I saw him, or his absence, in that spare room before they took his body away. I was just reaching the conclusion that the poem would never be finished, that it wasn't meant to be a poem at all, just a way of me thinking through the process of grieving. It had been left untitled, draft after draft, all this time. When I wrote the word 'Episodics' at the top of the latest failed attempt, it began to make sense – to me at least – of the slippage, the breakage.

—

By the time that poem had a title, I was working on another. This was a poem to be set by the composer Emily Howard, an experiment born out of Emily's interest in mathematics. Rather than start with an image, idea, phrase or tune, we would choose a number and work from there. Having spent so long trying to write about that final meeting with my father (or not him) three years before, I was glad of the chance to start with something more abstract. So we settled on eleven. It was angular, like the syllable counts

Marianne Moore used to set herself to push her poems into stranger, more idiosyncratic and unsettling shapes. And it felt freer. The poem could wander wherever it chose. I wanted to write about the loss of my mum, but that was too recent and more complicated. She had been leaving us – and herself – for many months, exacerbated by the time-warping repetition and isolation of the pandemic.

The world outside was losing its grip on chronology. In peak lockdown, the crab apple tree outside my window became a magic lantern. I'd always been glad of it, the only tree in our back garden, but that didn't stop me looking past, over, or in winter through it from the back bedroom where I work. Bullfinches, greenfinches, goldfinches, blue tits, coal tits, starlings would all land and sing and leave, land and sing and leave. They started to photobomb the poems I was supposed to be writing. Eleven. I went back to that. Keep it abstract as long as possible, see what comes of it. Eleven short sections. Maybe eleven lines each? No. Too long. When set for singers it would last for hours. Different line counts for each section, but eleven syllables a line. Worth a go. I started playing with images, riffs off the word 'eleven': elliptical, electric, heaven, even. I was three draft sections in when I started describing a fledgling, not yet cut loose, fragile and hopeless. The birds from the tree were pushing their way in. But this wasn't about the birds. As the image of the bird hardened on the draft page it became an image of an old woman dropped into a care-home cot like an overripe bruised fruit.

—

HYMN TO NOVEMBER

Strangers are tethered to dogs, or sit
in oversized and idling cars, or bear
heavy coats and bags as ballast.
I keep myself grounded with stones
in my pockets, marked with my children's names.

Yet this morning the city itself
could take off, under such blind winter sun.
Our words rise up in rapture,
and breath smokes like an offering.
Old stones recast as celestial.

Amid all this weightlessness, a beggar
strips in the street, wants out. No one helps.
There is no way to the soul
but through the body. A butcher hangs
a haunch inside his window. *Ave.*

—

In my early years of fascination with the *Quartet*, I never took much notice of the fifth movement. I knew it as well as all the other movements, but I tended to listen to the *Quartet* as a whole, from first to eighth movements. I always found it utterly beautiful and heartsore in its longing, but it didn't generate the pictures that I got from the mighty angel in the second section or the unforgettable bird-haunted abyss in section three. Messiaen's notes to number five are fuller than most, but more ethereal, stating its aim to magnify the eternal, powerful, gentle Word in music that extends into a 'tender, supreme distance'. In my notes, I've written 'what does this mean?' I realise this is crass of me. A painter friend once told me that whenever I came to his studio the paintings I said I liked were always the ones with human figures in them. I once wrote a book of poems called *Drysalter*, which took some bearings from the Psalms. It took some numbers from them too, as it consists of 150 poems of fifteen lines each. The poems are full of human figures, loved and wounded, dead and risen. A poem called 'Hymn to November' says 'There is no way to the soul / but through the body', which is as close to an *ars poetica* as I've come up with yet. It's personal. I think I also struggled with the word 'Louange'. It made me think of 'lounge' bars, particularly louche ones full of velvet, or crooners, or lizards, or suits. I've got nothing against lounging. But I sensed it wasn't the vision intended by the composer.

—

Messiaen's vision is a complex thing. His synaesthesia gives it a spin, but there's something in his music, and the way he talks about it, that attracts words like 'visionary' or 'mystic'. While acknowledging that some rare people have genuine mystical experiences, he was profoundly suspicious of such terms when applied to him. He preferred to characterise himself as orthodox and passionate about his faith. When you read about real mystics, it's not hard to see why Messiaen didn't want the term attached to him. Some of the Görlitz mystic Jakob Böhme's ideas – like his notion of seven essential energies of the universe, in two sets of three with the crucial *'Blitz'* or Flash connecting the two (no, me neither) – sit at the outer edges of the esoteric. This is part of the fascination for some of his followers, drawing up charts to demonstrate the interaction of the seven forces.

Like Messiaen in the *Quartet*, Böhme's writing is an attempt to step outside the constraints of time and space. And like listening to the *Quartet*, reading the writings of Böhme – notably in his *Aurora* – is a heady dance with order and chaos. Both works have a genesis story set in Görlitz: Messiaen's in 1941 in Stalag VIII-A and Böhme's in 1600 a couple of miles down the road by the River Neisse. Messiaen was not there by choice, but Böhme was trying to build a business, working as a shoemaker, married to a daughter of the local butcher and about to start a family. For such an expansive, abstract set of ideas, the genesis of Böhme's vision was surprisingly concrete and specific, like a Polaroid. It was an everyday moment of beauty – a recently polished pewter bowl, touched by a ray of sunlight – which caught his attention and held it. But in those moments of rapture he said the mysteries of the world were revealed to him: the true nature of God, the reasons for creation, the meaning of suffering and redemption, life beyond the end of time. It calls to mind for me the English mystic Julian of Norwich in the fourteenth century, with her own precisely framed Polaroid of a hazelnut in the palm of her hand, described by the poet Denise Levertov as 'the macrocosmic egg, sublime paradox, / brown hazelnut of All that Is—/ made, and belov'd, and preserved.'

—

The film-maker Andrei Tarkovsky was given a Polaroid camera by his friend the Italian director Michelangelo Antonioni in the 1970s when the 'instant camera' was a new invention. Tarkovsky was mesmerised by it and started taking photographs on his travels. For Tarkovsky, an artist obsessed by film-making as a way of 'sculpting in time', the Polaroid camera allowed him to freeze a scene into a solid object even as it vanished in linear time. He took them sparingly, but beautifully, curating his Polaroid images in a box he took with him everywhere, using these Polaroid prints as touchstones for his work. In recent years, Tarkovsky's Polaroids have been published, and they are remarkable, commonplace and numinous.

In 2016 a collection of these original images was put on sale at Bonhams in London in batches of six to nine prints, each with an estimate of £20,000–£30,000. Like painted icons they hold value in two worlds. I couldn't stretch to bid on the original prints, but the ones I've seen are as radiant and serene as icons. I can see why it would mean something to own the Polaroids themselves. Reputedly, he burnt the ones he felt had failed, curating his box of sacred images. These are everyday icons: the artist's wife stands by a fence looking out across scrub fields towards a house set in a copse, or his dog is caught mid-step on a garden path with an ochre sky behind and misted watercolour trees, or there's an empty hallway where a single window pours sunlight over two straight-back chairs. Quotidian stuff, but no less sacred for that.

Tarkovsky's 1975 *Mirror* is a film I've seen seven or eight times and the furniture keeps moving. It is regarded as the director's most autobiographical work, about an ageing writer facing the end of his life, dreaming and remembering scenes from his childhood, his marriage, incorporating some of Tarkovsky's father's own poetry. It is every bit as beautiful as his Polaroids, but what fascinates me most about it is the structure. It has been compared with 'stream-of-consciousness' narratives, but I think that's the wrong analogy. It has a strong internal structure, but the way time works in this film is more musical than narrative. It loops and echoes its images and phrases in the same way as the *Quartet*. To get these loops and structures right took Tarkovsky – by his own account – twenty-one complete re-edits of the film, and even by the twentieth he had no confidence that it would ever be finished. To his great relief in the edit suite, as the twenty-first version of *Mirror* came together, the director said in his filmic *ars poetica Sculpting in Time*: 'Time itself, running through the shots, had met and linked together.' I have, on the wall above my desk, a still from *Mirror*, a screenshot I had to keep rewinding and pausing to catch as the scene flew past. The picture frames a window with the figure of a mother staring out in silhouette. She looks down at the courtyard below where her young son is standing at a fire he has made. The flames make shadows on the walls. And there's a frozen line from the English subtitles at the foot of the screenshot, translating the Russian script as: 'A poet is called upon to provoke a spiritual jolt.'

—

Shadows and shades. Rather like hearing birdsong properly for the first time, I've been noticing shadows a lot these last few years. In *Mirror*, in all his films, in his Polaroids too, Tarkovsky is a choreographer of time and light. But architects have been working this way for centuries. Louis Kahn – designer of august civic structures like the Salk Institute in California and the National Assembly Building in Bangladesh – declared in 1960 that 'even a space intended to be dark should have just enough light from some mysterious opening to tell us how dark it really is. Each space must be defined by its structures and the character of its natural light.' It rings true, but the light does not have to be natural to transfigure, to offer glimpses of a world beyond the end of time. Tenebrae in the western Christian tradition is a liturgy which takes place at the end of Holy Week. It's a liturgy of darkness, in which music and readings are accompanied by the gradual extinguishing of candles. But the mystery and beauty of Tenebrae comes from shadows. Candles cast fragile, unstable patterns. There's a dance, a playfulness to their solemnity. It's no wonder the old word for a ghost was a shade, from the same root word. At Tenebrae, as the candles are put out one by one, the shadows shift perspective and shimmer, and the church or cathedral seems to come alive. I had an interest in these shadow dramas long before I had any time for their content.

As a Lancastrian, I see fewer shadows than most. Unless you count the rain shadows that my car leaves when I move it after yet another torrential night. Pale, northern children like me had to take their shadows where they could, lying on our backs in the street until the rain left a dry print of our bodies when we stood up. Then we watched as they darkened and disappeared. Shadows in childhood are a source of fear and fascination. On a bright day with low morning sun, the thrown or cast shadow looks like a child's work of art, a great loose-limbed spatter painting on a wall. I was never sure if we throw them, or they throw us. Seeing your shadow – in rain or sun – is salutary, comforting. If you can see your own shadow, it means you're not lying in it, as the dead tend to do. The folklore notion of the loss of a shadow as a harbinger of death is matched only by the horror of being fused with your shadow at the moment of death. The blast-shadows left on walls and streets, when the apogee of human destructive power made bodies vanish, leaving only the negative print of their final moment.

—

Japanese culture has, for centuries, challenged our western assumptions about light and shadows. In an essay by the novelist Junichiro Tanizaki, written in 1933 and translated under the title 'In Praise of Shadows', he tries to explain what he regards as a very un-western trait in his own culture, the propensity to seek beauty in shadows: 'The West too has known a time when there was no electricity, gas, or petroleum, and yet so far as I know the West has never been disposed to delight in shadows. Japanese ghosts have traditionally had no feet; Western ghosts have feet, but are transparent. As even this trifle suggests, pitch darkness has always occupied our fantasies, while in the West even ghosts are as clear as glass. This is true too of our household implements: we prefer colours compounded of darkness, they prefer the colours of sunlight.' He goes on to criticise the western ritual of polishing metal tableware 'to a glittering brilliance', praising instead the 'burnish and patina' of the unpolished bowl.

If he hadn't died over three centuries before Tanizaki's polemic, Jakob Böhme might have taken it personally. If the patina on that pewter bowl had gone unpolished, so the sun fell flat on its face, then perhaps Böhme would know nothing of the nature of God or humanity, of this world or the next. It makes me think I should pay more attention to these small daily rituals, as monastics are taught to do, in case the shine on a knife reveals the secrets of the universe.

At the end of his essay, Tanizaki issues a rallying cry to save what he calls 'this world of shadows we are losing', at least in literature if not in life. 'In this mansion called literature', he says, 'I would have the eaves deep and the walls dark, I would push back into the shadows the things that have come forward too clearly.'

—

A day at what was Mum and Dad's house, sizing up the task ahead of us. Now the funeral is done, we don't want the house and contents ceded to the dust, held unchanging like some macabre museum with everything exactly as it was on the night Mum had her fall. Need to get moving. How soon after death the morbid exigencies take over. I sit at the table, with a notebook and a phone. All curtains are drawn, cobwebs swag in doorways and from light fittings, traps set in every room. Go through the list of calls, helplines, how to close all their accounts, how to drain the tank and pipes, pull the plugs, block off the gas. Draw the house back to its elements – brick, plaster, drawers and cupboards stuffed with relics: tickets, pocket diaries, bills from closed accounts. This house is all shadow now.

It is not our childhood home. They moved here to be nearer us, to see more of their grandchildren. But when they moved they brought their accidental archive with them. Their lives – our childhoods – collected, uncurated, stored in case it might be of some future use, some interest. Every room was packed, stacked high. The garage floor-to-ceiling full of stuff they knew that they would never need again, in boxes marked with 'old clothes' or 'crockery'. Half-posthumous, these stacks, the garage a waiting room for objects to pass from one generation to the next, or into skips. They cannot have imagined we would keep all this.

—

And what about them? Are their shades here? I was dreading turning the key, stepping into the hallway. I don't know if that dread was fear of absence or of presence.

—

A bright day casts longer, stronger shadows. It is because we are incarnate, embodied, that we obstruct the light. For a philosopher and mystic like Simone Weil, this was a problem. She longed to achieve a sort of transparency, so that her creator could look right through her: 'I cannot conceive the necessity for God to love me, when I feel so clearly that even with human beings affection for me can only be a mistake. But I can easily imagine that he loves that perspective of creation which can only be seen from the point where I am. But I act as a screen. I must withdraw so that he may see it. I must withdraw so that God may make contact with the beings whom chance places in my path and whom he loves. It is tactless for me to be there. It is as though I were placed between two lovers or two friends.'

Simone Weil's life can be read as an attempt at that transparency she craved. She was born in Paris in 1909 to a secular Jewish family, and it's fair to say she was intellectually precocious. In fact, given that her only sibling, André, became one of the twentieth century's greatest mathematicians, you wouldn't want to be in their class at school. Simone Weil's works in philosophy, political theory and theology have been as influential as her brother's mathematics, but she was far from a conventional academic. At the Sorbonne in Paris, she was regarded as a genius by her professors and her fellow students. One of those fellow students was Simone de Beauvoir, who in her own memoirs described Weil sweeping through the quadrangle followed by a trail of acolytes, with a book of philosophy in each pocket of her long, dark-grey overall. 'I envied her for having a heart that could beat right across the world,' said de Beauvoir of Weil's response to a famine in China, but when the two Simones met it didn't go well: 'She declared in no uncertain terms', said de Beauvoir, 'that only one thing mattered in the world today – the revolution which would feed all the starving people of the earth. I retorted, no less peremptorily, that the problem was not to make men happy, but to find the reason for their existence. She looked me up and down: "It's easy to see you've never gone hungry," she snapped.' That was the end of their relationship, but in the final exams they led the philosophy cohort, with Weil first and de Beauvoir second.

To call Weil an activist is to redefine the term. Her response to suffering and injustice was to eliminate any gap between belief and life, even if this led to personal disaster. She didn't just protest and advocate for improvements in the lives of factory workers, she became one, leaving academia to get a job on the factory floor in a Renault car plant. When the Spanish Civil War broke out, she signed up to fight for the anarchist side on the front line, and later worked as a farm labourer. By her own admission she was ill-equipped for these challenges. Physically weak and myopic, she was sent home from Spain with burns after tripping over a cooking pot almost as soon as she arrived. Her debilitating headaches, seemingly untreatable, made her daily life an exercise in endurance.

To call her a mystic requires some redefining too. Yet in her key spiritual encounter in the abbey at Solesmes she was contemplating the meaning of George Herbert's poem 'Love' when, as she later put it, 'Christ himself came down and took possession of me.' She was completely unprepared for this experience, but did not doubt its authenticity. In fact, she remarked that God had been a step ahead in preventing her, in her vast and wide reading, from looking at any of the writings of mystics 'so that it should be evident to me that I had not invented the absolutely unexpected contact'. Her secular political philosophy had been rooted in endless rigorous questioning of her own – and others' – assumptions and intentions. So it was with her mystical encounters.

—

I came across Weil's work in my twenties, a few years after I first heard the *Quartet*, through the political scientist

David McLellan's biography *Utopian Pessimist*. It's more than an account of the life, it's a distilled and generous introduction to her thought too. I'm not the first poet to see this fascinating and infuriating philosopher-mystic as a poet too. Her work is hard to cast as a systematic philosophy, not least because she died young and left her work in articles, essays, lectures and correspondence rather than a series of books. But her influences were as wide-ranging as her interests, so for me the best of her posthumously published work is her notebooks. Unedited, personal, passionate and scattergun in their focus, these books are full of short, metaphorical thought experiments and aphorisms. I remember being struck, at first reading, by her notion of attention, the focused act of waiting on God, a form of creative self-denial or self-emptying. And she's a genius of the paradox. It was a provocation to my then atheism to read her argument that non-believers may be closer to God than believers, as the God conjured by believers is bound to be a pale shadow of the truth.

—

But yes, reading those prose poems, thought experiments, whatever they were, I remember as I read each one how it would open in my head like a Rose of Jericho. Some still do, like this one from her posthumous collection 'Gravity and Grace': 'Two prisoners whose cells adjoin communicate with each other by knocking on the wall. The wall is the thing which separates them but it is also their means of communication. It is the same with us and God. Every separation is a link.'

—

Messiaen and Weil are miles apart in many ways: the faithful composer who was born believing, born a musician too, never questioned the fundamentals of either, and the restless, reckless philosopher-mystic-activist. But to my mind they are formed of the same stuff – both expansive and voracious in their range of interests and influences, both bold and experimental in the way they make their work, both utterly committed to their work. I've never come across an account of the two of them meeting, though there was some overlap in their intellectual circles in Paris, which is enough for me to imagine a short (probably unwatchable) film in which they meet at a cafe near the Sorbonne to discuss the meaning of life. It opens with a minute's silence – the caped philosopher chain-smoking and the beret-and-scarfed composer sipping coffee as he taps out non-retrogradable rhythms on the tablecloth – then a solid hour of them discussing their favourite crystals. That's the other thing they share, both contrary enough to confound an imaginary film-maker's designs on their conversation.

—

Now I've read more about the roots of *Quartet*'s fifth movement, the water spectacle on the Seine for which Messiaen employed the sci-fi keening of the ondes martenot, I can't un-hear the ondes. The syrupy, glorious cello part – marked by the composer as 'ecstatic' – retains an echo of the ondes but turns it into an other-worldly eulogy. The only punctuation is the piano's gentle, stuttering heartbeat under it, then as the cello fades out, this pulse falters too – a run of eight beats, then six, then four – all on the same chord, until it stops. It was only when I first saw *Quartet* played live, after decades of listening to recordings, that I heard the piano as the toll of a bell.

Messiaen's notes on the score for the *Quartet*, to guide the players beyond what is set out in the dots on the page, are remarkable in themselves. They are no doubt maddening, at times, for the players – as in his 'infinitely slow' instruction to the cellist – but as a listener they are wonderful, notes for us as much as for the four musicians on the stage. Imagine reading the note 'ecstatic and paradisic' instructing you to play in a way that invokes prelapsarian glory. Or 'vigorous, granite-like, and a bit fast'. Or 'extremely slow and tender'. Or 'like a bird'. Or best of all, 'with love'.

—

Simone Weil's longing for transparency, no more to block that gaze between creator and created, reached a terrible apotheosis at the age of thirty-four. Having fled occupied

Paris for New York – worried for the safety of her parents – she had travelled to England to prepare for a return to France to work with the Resistance. As ever, she wanted an active physical role behind the lines. But de Gaulle and the Free French gave her an intellectual, strategic role instead, keeping her in London to draw up plans for a new post-war France. In particular, she developed a plan for front-line nurses to tend to the wounds of combatants in the heat of battle. This was not intended solely to offer better, swifter treatment, but for the nurses to exemplify self-sacrificial love in direct contrast to Nazi cruelty. Like her wish to be sent on sabotage missions behind the lines, this plan was not enacted.

The story of Weil's last few months is a bleak one. A collapse in London, diagnosis of TB and confinement in a sanatorium in Ashford, Kent. Once there, though her TB was regarded as curable on admission, she ate too little to regain her strength or to fight the bacilli. Her strict moral logic meant she would not eat more than the poor in occupied France whose rations were reportedly meagre. McLellan describes this as 'communion with France by natural abstention' adding that 'it seems probable that she had developed a disorder of her digestive system' which made eating difficult and painful. Nonetheless, the coroner's report stated that 'the deceased did kill and slay herself by refusing to eat whilst the balance of her mind was disturbed'. In that light, her death looks like a terrible form of self-abnegation, a disappearing act.

—

Inspired by Tarkovsky's Polaroids, I bought, off a friend, an instant camera. He had taken and printed one image of me on the day he bought it, then he put the camera back in its case and never used it again. I've had it about six months now and I haven't taken a single shot. When my sister and I cleared out our parents' house, we found boxes and boxes and boxes of photographs stacked up in the garage, each with hundreds of paper wallets stuffed with negatives and prints. They never stuck them in albums, nor got them out to reminisce. They were not labelled or dated or noted on the flip side of the prints. I don't think they were there for us or for the grandchildren, because so many contain places, faces, dates that are impossible to relocate. My dad, in particular, who was organised enough to list items in cupboards and to leave a file called 'when we go', would surely have cut them down and marked them up if he wanted us to keep them as a time capsule. I think the taking and developing of pictures was a ritual, a liturgy to be carried out at Christmas, weddings and christenings, especially on holidays or day trips. To take a camera and run through a roll of film was how you knew you were breaking your routines. The point never was to keep an archive. Nonetheless they didn't chuck out the boxes in the garage. And now they are in my garage instead.

The same could be said of my own Polaroids, though I appear to have pushed the ritual a stage further by not taking any shots at all. Maybe my pointless sound archive serves the same end. Tracks of birds, attempts to record seals on rocks off the coast of Northumberland, recordings of walks through busy streets, of a waterfall in the Peak District, announcements on a train. They are not even good recordings, most of them. I like them best when there's an audible shadow, some instrument running through scales in the next street, or an incoherent conversation on a parallel path, the audio penumbra. Maybe these can fulfil the role of shade, white-outs and blurs in a curated box of Polaroids. I like the idea of impure sound recording – though it may be self-justification for ineptitude – a parallel to Louis MacNeice's 'impure poetry' conditioned by the particularities and messiness of the poet's life and the place and time in which the poems are written. It's the sacrament of the present moment.

—

For the young winged man Icarus as his feet disappear into the sea, the seconds he spent in his plunge from the sun were of a different pace entirely from the tired daydreaming ploughman or the idly grazing sheep. Bruegel's land, sea or snowscapes are arresting not just because of their ordinariness, their humanity, but also their exposure of time as dependent entirely upon perspective. It's no surprise that Andrei Tarkovsky saw Bruegel as a key influence. In a 1979 interview, Tarkovsky said he had created, in *Mirror*, two or three shots of 'the boy, the small silhouettes of men, the snow, the bare trees and the river in the distance', with a conscious intent to honour the painter whose work he so loved and admired. His films can be stopped at almost any point and they look like paintings. Not always Bruegels, though some of the winter wide-shots do. Sometimes they look like Renaissance portraits or icons, or domestic interiors by a Vermeer or a Vuillard. His Polaroids don't look like paintings at all though. Not to me at least.

—

I've noticed, on recent viewings, that Tarkovsky's films are full of birdsong. I heard a story years ago that for his film *Nostalghia* the director wanted to use Messiaen's *Quatuor* on the soundtrack. It's not there in the final cut, and I haven't been able to back up the story, but I like to think it's true.

—

I have looked for Simone Weil in Paris, in the course of making a radio feature about her. Or rather, I've looked for a trace, a momentary slippage between past and present, a brush of her cloak in the quadrangle of the École Normal Supérieure between the box hedges and slender trees. Nothing. Likewise in the street by the Luxembourg Gardens where the Weil family lived, marked by a plaque. Not even in the Bibliothèque Nationale with one of her notebooks marked with tiny precise handwriting and decorated with Sanskrit texts and drawings. Not a shade of her anywhere. To her friend Simone Deitz, she wrote: 'Like me, you are a piece that God has cut out badly. But I soon will no longer be cut out; I shall be re-attached and united.'

—

SIMONE'S LAST AND FIRST

If the first thing you saw was not the flaky
ceiling of your parents' Boulevard de Strasbourg
    home,
nor the red upside-down face of Mme Zeitlin,
the grim midwife, then it must have been before –
a streak of light that tempted you, pulled
you into the huge, firm hands.

If the last thing you saw was not the ivory
glint from an August afternoon on a drip-marked
sink in the sanatorium – taps poised, pipes like roots
in search of water – then there may never be one.
All we see is a lit taper, as much as we can take,
before light overcomes us.

CHAPTER 6

Furious Dance for the Seven Trumpets

A wild flailing, trumpets, stone music, great granite sheets sounding, hurtling steel, a fury of purple, a drunkenness of ice.

—

Not for the first time, for this listener, Messiaen's notes for the sixth section are enticing and inconceivable. He talks of the music as stone-like, then specifies terrifying and sonorous granite. Steel on the move, unstoppable. Vast blocks of purple fury. A head-spinning icy intoxication. He then invites the listener to focus especially on the 'terrible fortissimo' of the theme at the end of the piece. The composer's title for this section is 'Danse de la fureur, pour les sept trompettes'. And it is a furious dance indeed. He described it as the most 'rhythmically characteristic' of the sections (more on those rhythms later) and to my ear it is a crazy chase, with occasional screaming halts and restarts, handbrake turns and gear shifts. Relentless in pursuit of its melodic line, it must feel like a fury for the players too, since it is the only section in the *Quartet* played entirely in unison. Anthony Pople said it presents 'a fearsome challenge to performers'.

—

I wish I could say that my first thought, reading Messiaen's description of 'sept trompettes', against a background of stone and steel, was the Book of Revelation that was his primary source for the descriptions. In truth, my first thought was a colossal retail mall on the banks of the Manchester Ship Canal. Some musical purists mistook Messiaen's full-bodied, throw-it-all-in, odes-martenot-powered *Turangalila Symphony* for the melodies of a bordello. Some architectural purists mistake the Trafford Centre's Mancunian 'drunkenness of things being various' for a Coleridgean nightmare without the opiates. When I think of angels with trumpets now, I do think of the Book of Revelation, and of Messiaen's *Quartet*, and of the entrance to the Trafford Centre. To be fair, it is quite an entrance: colonnades and rooftop statuary, angels with long trumpets standing or reclining as they play, while others welcome you with laurels held above a vast stone unicorn, rearing horses, roaring lions. A giant griffin leans off the roof towards the bronze and glass doors where the words 'hold fast to that which is good' (from the biblical Epistle to the Thessalonians) are carved into the architrave.

In Xanadu, for all its treasures and excess, there was a counterweight – measurelessness, the shadow side of caves and voids, for every jewel a clump of pitch, for each grand hall alive with noise there was a silent cavern. To see behind this Trafford *trompe l'oeil* you find an unmarked door, walk through into the grey, the ante-space, the blank page on which colours coalesce. On this shadow side, the corridors close in, the ceiling gets lower. The light side of the centre is so full of human bodies, trees and plants, that even when you expect an echo it's minimal. Here is where the echo comes to hide, in the vast network of service and evacuation corridors.

My favourite myth about this inverse pleasure dome conjures an unlit marble hall somewhere away from public access, where unused statues stand in serried rows waiting for the call. I like to picture them pressed together marble heels to marble toes: the nymphs with hands outstretched for waterfalls, the Caesars, goddesses, crowd-pleasers, water-bearers, garland-wearers, the timid and the brave out of Tuscany, Arcady, alchemy, fantasy. Angels of the apocalypse awaiting vacant plinths, where they can stand on the roof in rain and snow, lift their trumpets to their lips and blow.

—

I keep going back to the last few hours in that hospital room, wondering whether or not Mum could hear us, regretting not holding her hand. When I arrived, her arms were tucked in tight by the blankets on the bed. I guess they may have worried she might pull off her oxygen mask, or had to comply with Covid restrictions. How often since I've wished I had untucked the hand on my side and held it. We did stroke her hair, kissed her (through a mask... why on earth did I not take it off?) but I should have held her hand, felt the warmth, her faltering pulse. Is it usual for the heart not to stutter and stop but to keep beating, more and more faintly like the slowest fade-out, so the nurse has to lean in, shut his eyes to concentrate to try to find it in the wrist, the neck? It changed my sense of the heart, that night. It's still the symbol of difference between life and death, still full of longing. For all its messy truth as a bruise-coloured loosely fist-shaped pump, it still has endless representations as a stylised cordate shape with two smooth curves at the top and a point at the base. Cordate gets tangled in my head with cordite, which is a kind of explosive. But now I've come to think of it as a very slow fade-out.

—

The historian Fay Bound Alberti, in her book *This Mortal Coil*, tells the probably apocryphal story of the poet Shelley's cremation after his accidental drowning. His body was reduced to ashes – the legend goes – except for his heart, which survived the flames and was rescued from the pyre, to be kept and treasured – wrapped in silk – by his grieving wife. One of the aspects of Alberti's work on the heart that really struck me was her account of medical students who were interviewed after they had performed dissections on human hearts. Compared with dissecting brains or other organs, the handling of a human heart seemed to many of them to be a privilege, something to approach with special reverence. For many of us, the heart is not just the seat of emotions, but in some profound sense the seat of our selves. But at the root of all these metaphorical references to the heart is its central function – the beat, the repeated act on which we all rely, the heart's deceptively simple signature move that functions as the source of life and a key metaphor for it. We are alive because it keeps beating, keeps measuring out our minutes and seconds. It is nothing if not restless.

—

EXCISE ME

So shattered is my heart from endless
pounding at my chest wall to get out,
that I give in one summer dawn and cut
then lift it. Cupped in my hands
like a half-caught bird, it cools and stills.

I place it on the sill to keep it warm,
and lie down on my bed to take stock
of this new thoracic calm. Hours pass,
then weeks. The sun through glass

dries my heart into a peach stone.

Another day, I think, just one more
to be sure I will recall this stasis so deep
I can hear huge clouds of blind fish
under ice-sheets, spiders in the leaf-mould
of distant forests, your thoughts.

—

The most rhythmically characteristic movement of the set. That's this sixth section. Messiaen's notes then highlight 'the use of added values, augmented or diminished rhythms, and non-retrogradable rhythms', whatever they might be. At this point, it seems timely to set out my own musical credentials. I had one year of learning the piano starting at age five and a half. I remember getting as far as 'out of the desert the cowboy did ride / see the [can't remember, probably a gun] down by his side'. Then I remember being so bored by the lessons that I persuaded – i.e. whined and pestered – my parents to let me give up. My mum, incidentally, took piano lessons as a child in Salford, and got further than me. She had a better excuse for giving up too. She lived a few streets away from another pupil called Peter, who had the lesson immediately before hers on a weekday after school. She would pass Peter – a shy, withdrawn child, she said – on the pavement outside, then go in for a half-hour of failure and being told how good Peter was. He grew up to be the composer Sir Peter Maxwell Davies, after which she felt vindicated.

In my early teens at the local comprehensive we were told we could skip lessons once a week to learn an instrument, which seemed like a good deal. I chose the trumpet, but all I remember learning was the word embouchure and the way it made your lips go numb. I do remember opening the old trumpet case from the school store, with its tattered purple velvet lining and the smell of metal polish. Those lessons lasted two terms. From my brief experiments with brass, I am confident that the Trafford Centre angels would need supernatural abilities to recline on one side like that and still get a tune out of a fanfare trumpet.

In my late teens I was in local bands playing (mainly) David Bowie covers. In these bands I was always the singer, largely on the grounds that I couldn't play an instrument. For about five years in my early forties I was part of a function band playing wedding receptions, birthday parties, fundraisers and the like, with four other middle-aged men who had been in bands in their youth and wanted to experience that buzz again. One of our guitarists had a day job as a music producer so we recorded an album – private distribution only, all copies accounted for – but it fizzled out when we determined that no hat yet created can disguise the ravages of time. That's it. At least, that's the extent of my formal music education. Alongside that, I've had a parallel life as an obsessive listener and collector (though I've stopped buying vinyl since everybody is at it now) and in a recent party game I concluded that the reason I forget things is because my memory is entirely full of song lyrics I can recite within the first three seconds of any track from the last five decades.

As a poet and librettist, I've worked for three decades with composers and musicians to write texts for song cycles, choral works, oratorios and operas. They know I never learnt to read an orchestral score, but I still feel embarrassed in rehearsal rooms, turning the pages when everyone else does, rather than declining the offer of a reading copy and simply listening. The dots on the page are mesmerising though, and there have been times when I've picked up a thread and followed.

In recent years, the two composers I've worked with most frequently – James MacMillan and Emily Howard – have talked to me about Messiaen from their perspectives. They both share my fascination with his music. His name came up again when I met a young composer on a residency in Germany and mentioned that I was writing about *Quartet for the End of Time*. Oh wow, he said. That piece. Whenever I think about musical time I go back and study the score. It changed everything. I asked him something about non-retrogradable rhythms, and he said yes, what Messiaen does with those rhythms is extraordinary.

—

So it was that I bought the full score of *Quatuor pour la fin du temps* from the legendary French music publisher Éditions Durand, plus the four separate instrumental parts. Then I fixed up meetings with James and Emily, to sit down with each of them and spread out the score so they could explain what a non-retrogradable rhythm might be. And why it matters.

—

It is a Friday evening in early March. James is on his way back from a trip south and calls in to see us. We go out for dinner at the Bangladeshi restaurant round the corner, where we've got into the pattern – bad for pounds of both kinds – of eating every Friday evening when we're at home. Over South Indian murghi, I tell James I'm writing about my love of *Quatuor pour la fin du temps* and that I want to talk to him about Messiaen's approach to musical time. I mention non-retrogradable rhythms and my need to understand what they are and why the composer uses them. And I want to hear about Messiaen's other spins on musical time, its loops and its end. I get out the score and set it in front of him.

Nine months later I meet up with Emily. It's early on a cold winter Sunday morning. Despite my possibly unwise decision to get the scores out over South Indian murghi in March, Emily and I are sitting in a cafe in December where the tables are a bit too tight for comfort. We spread out Éditions Durand's wares across our half of the table. A mother and daughter sharing the table with us move their coffee cups to give us more space. They say it sounds interesting, the *Quartet for the End of Time*, and I say yes it is. But I don't mention non-retrogradable rhythms. The cafe is filling up fast with dog-walkers, night workers, the heavy-eyed in need of carbs. This is the first cafe to open on a Sunday and the breakfast smells good.

In the interests of musical (if not narrative) clarity, I will combine the restaurant in spring with the cafe in winter to create an imaginary giant table on which two huge scores of the *Quartet* are open and two composers are trying to explain it to a poet sitting on the other side trying to decide whether to eat dinner or breakfast:

'Non-retrogradable rhythms. It's hard to explain. It's a rhythm that can't be turned back on itself. So it generates its own strange pulse.' James points at the score on the table. 'I mean, that's one duration. That's another duration. That's another duration. That's the same as that duration.' I say, 'Right, right.' He points at the score again. 'So in fact, if you look at the score here, that little sort of birdy thing that we call a dotted quaver [he knows my musical education consisted of a few piano lessons at the age of six plus a brief blast on the trumpet in my early teens], then a crotchet tied to a semiquaver, followed by a minim, and then it goes into reverse. And so there's a kind of palindromic rhythmic thing going on. He's thinking about how to control and manipulate musical time in a very, very different way from, say, the German Romantics, who wouldn't give this a second thought.' This is good. This is what I needed. 'He gets this from raga. He gets it from the kind of Indian classical music that he was interested in, which is saturated by this. There's a similar kind of palindrome thing going on there.'

He points to the score again. It's upside down to me

and the pickle tray is partially obscuring it. 'See, it goes into reverse. And the same thing there. There's a kind of mirror image. So he's working on that basis all the time. Almost second nature to him. So this is being repeated across a series of chords, I can't remember how many, about thirty-odd chords. Then he starts it again. So in essence, you're talking about a very repetitive music, which doesn't feel repetitive.' He looks up. Right. Yes. I'm nodding. 'Because the rhythms and the durations are different the second time around. And then we'll have another time. Where does it start again? Here? There's the chords again, the shapes. And already the values are different.'

'So, do you know what a major scale is?' Emily too knows the extent of my musical training. Yeah, I know what a major scale is. She sings one. The people at the next table have got their food now. It smells fantastic. Emily is explaining Messiaen's 'modes of limited transposition'. Essentially, how he constructs harmonies. He works with seven 'modes', or variations on scales. These are the building blocks of his music. Their 'limited transposition' means that you can transpose each mode up a semitone (i.e. up to the note next to it) and the scale works, then again another semitone, likewise, and again, but with these seven particular modes, at some point they will come round to the same note you began with. Emily says that though many composers have used some of these modes, Messiaen devises 'a kind of massive method', mapped out in his book *La technique de mon langage musical*. These seven modes of limited transposition then, what difference do they make to the music? 'It just opens up a lot of different possibilities,' says Emily. 'If I hear Messiaen's chords, they're so remarkably unique or idiosyncratic, you can tell it's Messiaen immediately.' I need another coffee. Or a Cobra beer.

To the untrained eye (I have two of those) it is hard to pick out these modes in the score because 'not only is he doing them, he's also putting them into time signatures'. Ah, time. Yes. What does he do with time? Emily chooses section six, in which we offer the seven trumpets a furious dance, to talk about Messiaen and time. 'This section is so hard to play because it's all four players in unison the whole way through. They do exactly the same thing. It's quite an amazing piece, right?' It is. James said in this movement Messiaen had made the four players into one meta-instrument. 'It's a very simple idea,' he said. 'But a very brave thing to do.'

'So can you see this?' I can. Emily is pointing at the score for section six. 'Okay. So quaver quaver quaver semiquaver, quaver quaver quaver, that's non-retrogradable. Do you understand the principle of that?' I think I do. 'So if you played it backwards, it might sound different because there are different tones and notes attached to it, but rhythmically it would be the same.' James mentioned palindromes. And now I get it. Messiaen employs these loops in harmony (the modes of limited transposition) and tempo (non-retrogradable rhythms) as a hidden architecture in *Quartet*. The piece is full of rhythmic palindromes. As Emily puts it, 'There is a pattern, but as a listener you can't quite grasp it, which is sort of perfect.' I wonder how it feels to be inside this musical time machine. What is it like for the players?

'Notice he doesn't have a time signature because it's too complicated. Maybe if you had an orchestra, you would have to, but because it's a chamber ensemble, it's easier not to. So what he does is he puts bar lines, the bar lines in this music, they don't mean every bar has the same number of beats, which is kind of standard. What it means is that every bar has . . . "this is a helpful place to think of a little break" somehow.'

—

Messiaen, in conversation, would bemoan the fact that we human beings are prisoners of rhythm. He would express frustration at the rhythmic predictability of our movement as bipedal animals, always the same walk one-two-one-two-one-two. When I came across his 'prisoners of rhythm' line I was a radio producer during the period of transition in editing, from marking up quarter-inch tapes with wax pencils and cutting them with razor blades, into the era of cut and paste on screen. The key to editing speech to keep it sounding natural was rhythm. There is just as much rhythm to speech as there is to poems – which often work with the rhythms of speech – or to music.

The one thing I missed when we ditched the now redundant skills of manual tape editing was the hands-on (literally, on the two spools) play with rhythm and pace. The slightest change of pace changes the rhythm of language, and the frequency changes with it, so you could manually slow a voice or speed it up and listen to strange pitches and nuances. I was reading at that time about Messiaen's obsession with rhythm and frequency, his sense of wonder at the sheer speed and virtuosity of birdsong, his need to slow it right down to make that music accessible to us. His line about rhythm got stuck in my head, then went into a notebook, then got mixed up with my day job sound-editing and came out in a poem.

—

THE FREQUENCY

This could be an explanation:
why we hear trees as wash and sibilance,
but swallows hear one thread
of a polyphony, an invitation.

Does the dusk call them down,
or vice versa? Plumping on wires like
ripe fruit, bluebirds darken into blackbirds,
and their talk weighs heavy

as the air swells with water. Even
the first rain has a voice as it begins its fall,
long before it breaks across
radio masts, roof gardens, cairns.

It strikes a note too high for us,
though animals with sharper ears
do look up at the song, and lean for cover.

QUARTET FOR THE END OF TIME

You're a prisoner of rhythm.

I believe that. Night falls now,
and under lightlessness I listen
for the footfalls of God in the garden.
The cool of evening is the time

he walked beneath the boughs of Eden,
softly, with his lips dried shut.
The apple was gone, man and woman
with it, and already

the bass tones of birdsong
were becoming shrill, sonorities
of breeze in grass were turning
into whispers. This was the fall of sound,

a rise in frequency, which rendered Paradise
inaudible. An army
of recordists could remind us what we lost,
could tape and slow by half,

then half again, then half, until we hear
the moans of distant suns like whale song,
until human voices slow to growls
and ratchet to a standstill.

Then – *shock* – our own breath,
when its pitch is slowed contains
the uncensored language of the heart,
yes words, our every sigh gives us away.

—

For clarinettist Kate Romano, who has just joined us at our imaginary hybrid table now, the hidden architecture of the *Quartet*'s score described by Emily and James is a help to players when you are trying to learn it: 'As a student, when I first played this piece, I remember thinking, "Oh, there's an extra quaver there . . . and one less there . . . ah, I see what he's done." And it's a very logical easy-on-the-eye way of notating it; if you just play what you see, it flows very naturally. Good musical grammar; it looks like what it is. Notating it in any other way would be nonsensical and unhelpful.'

Poems have hidden architecture too. Patterns of musicality – slant-rhymes and echoes, alliterations and rhythms – can be instinctive (by ear) on the part of the poet, but there are more consciously wrought structures too, like Gerard Manley Hopkins's mining of Anglo-Saxon forms and the sound of woven Welsh *cynghanedd* lines, his championing of 'sprung rhythm' as a way of granting the liberty of limit to poems in speech rhythms. Or Marianne Moore's bespoke modernist syllable-counts, shaping her stanza's syllabic measures that change in every line, her palindromic rhyme schemes. A buried architecture makes the poems feel intuitive, even impulsive, but also complete, as if their utterances had always been in those shapes, only waiting to be written down.

And is this looping, this particular pattern of repetition, something that's unusual in composers? James says it is. 'I can't think of anyone else who did it until that time. He introduced a new concept. If you look at the cello part, this is repetitive too. So he's got a handful of notes that keep repeating over and over again, but with different durations. And if you put that repetitive pattern on top of this kind of double repetitive pattern, you're getting a music of repeats, music of a static sensation, but it's not repetitive. It's continually on the move in a very, very strange and indeed mysterious way. And then he does the same kind of thing with the clarinet part. And the violin part. They're all looping round like the old technique of tape loops, where you would cut out a bit of tape and put it on an old reel-to-reel recorder, and it would just keep looping, looping, looping. Lots of bands did it.' He mentions the Bee Gees. I'm thinking of 10cc in 'I'm Not In Love'. Perhaps the use of tape loops in rock and pop was pioneered by Mancunian musicians. I like to think so. 'Well, Messiaen is doing that, but with live forms, live instruments, live players.' Right. Wow. 'And this is a pointer to his revolutionary view of musical time, which gives this piece its very specific character, because it's there for a reason. It's not there just as an aesthetic choice or simply as a rhythmic device. He is thinking theologically.'

—

Listening to the *Quartet* now, or picking my way slowly through the score, I can picture its veins and capillaries, sinews and muscles and lacework of bones, as intricate and complex as a bird in flight. But in *Quatuor pour la fin du temps* this temporal body is not just musical in intent, it is mystical. 'You're getting the sense of music repeating itself, but in a strangely non-repetitive way,' says James. 'He's presenting a vision of time that is revolutionary, that is outside of time. So it's his way of presenting God's time, which is separate from our time. It's a way of encapsulating at an almost subconscious level that God's time is forever. Messiaen is expressing something of the nature of God.'

—

It seems counter-intuitive for a composer to put the words 'Seven Trumpets' in the title of a piece of music played in unison by a violinist, cellist, clarinettist and pianist, but not a whiff of brass. Yet in his notes he implies that the four instruments together suggest trumpets – early on in this section – and later even a hint of gongs. I confess I've never noticed this. Over the years I've heard most commercially available recordings of the *Quartet*. I call up two versions now and put their takes on section six back to back on a playlist: a Deutsche Grammophon recording from 2000 (with Gil Shaham, Paul Meyer, Jian Wang and Myung-Whun Chung) regarded by some critics as the best to date, and that landmark recording made in Paris in 1956 and recently reissued, with Messiaen himself at the piano and Étienne Pasquier reprising his role as violinist from the Görlitz premiere, along with André Vacellier and Étienne's brother Jean.

The 1956 version, with the composer playing and presiding, has been seen as authoritative by some, but Rebecca Rischin points out that some of the tempi seem at odds with the score. My two recordings of this sixth section seem to back that up, as 'Furious Dance for the Seven Trumpets' is a lot less furious in 1956 (6'58") than it is in 2000 (5'40"). The more recent version is a breathtaking high-wire act, leaving me as a non-player wondering how it's actually possible for four instruments to play such complex music in unison at such a speed. And to summon the shades of (yes!) trumpets and gongs while they're doing it. The dynamic range is a revelation to me too. Switching from the full crazed dance to a ghostly echo on the cut of a bar line. I find it intoxicating. It's a racket, then when it turns into its own ghost it is a kind of ecstatic agony. I want the fury when I'm listening to the ghost, and the ghost when I'm listening to the fury. Messiaen is, I think, composing the silences between the movements too. They are all different, depending on the way he leads you in and out of them. It's as if he is retuning your ears as a listener in these seven hiatuses. At the end of this explosive sixth movement delivered by its 'meta-instrument', the silence leading into the seventh movement is a chasm.

—

Not far from where I live, and visible from the hills as far away as the Peak District, a giant ear strains night and day to try to catch a whisper from some distant star. Okay, it's not an ear, and it's not – strictly speaking – listening, but the Lovell radio telescope at Jodrell Bank has been tilting at distant stars since the late 1950s. Its moon-face tilts at this or that star or constellation, straining to pick up the tiniest trace of a message, some sign of life, perhaps from a distant galaxy. But for all its state-of-the-art technology, Jodrell Bank has a problem much closer to home.

The signals it is trying to tease out of the empty skies are easily drowned out by the dance of electronic fury we create around it. Even a mobile phone in a car on a nearby road can ruin it. Such fragile and difficult listening is constantly under threat. Whenever I've been near it, I've always been paranoid that a text or news alert hitting my phone might interfere with the fragile first attempt of a distant civilisation to contact humanity. It would be a shame if my sons' efforts to keep me posted on football transfer rumours meant we missed an incoming call from a distant galaxy.

The image conjured by Jodrell Bank is that of a universe of deep silence, with us as an island of noise, and the scientists trying desperately to listen for other such islands that may or may not exist countless light years away. It's a humbling image too, reminiscent of the line from Yeats's early poem 'The Song of the Happy Shepherd': 'The wandering earth herself may be / Only a sudden flaming word, / In clanging space a moment heard, / Troubling the endless reverie.' I read that image for the first time in my teens (the first Yeats poem I read) and it's stuck with me. I read Yeats's lines there as a version of 'you are dust, and to dust you shall return'.

We must clear the house. Every time we go it has retreated into deeper silence. I brought a radio with me to fill it. Anything that no one in the family wants will be offered to local charities, hospice, etc., but they tend to need very high safety specs, including fire-resistant material, etc., so I'm not sure how much will be of use to them. The rest goes to a house-clearance company. It's hard, carving up our parents' lifetime of possessions like this, including items of furniture they loved. Nothing is of any real financial value, but a lot of it was valuable to them and is associated with our childhood. My sister and I are trying to be logical, practical – although we sometimes waver. Every now and again one of us will say 'I'll have Dad's desk if you don't want it', or a table from our childhood home, or a chest of drawers, but then a few days later we've measured up and don't have room for it.

The strange feeling of sifting through the traces of their lives, and ours as children. They must have kept almost everything – so here were mountains of photographs, cards we made for Mother's Day and Father's Day, letters we wrote from school trips, school reports (ours, theirs, their parents') and vast piles of notebooks and diaries and books of lists. Two things we found in the upstairs dresser, while emptying it out, were an old autograph book of Mum's and a batch of letters. The autograph book was from her childhood, with messages, short rhymes and drawings by members of her family and friends, no one famous, just the people close to her. It's a lovely, obviously treasured book. The batch of letters is unsettling, not because it's troubling in content. The reverse, in fact. I only read a couple but they were written every day, one a day, from Dad to Mum when they were separated by work. Their youth, their sense of love and passion for each other, their excitement at standing on the threshold of their adult lives together, is wonderful, but just too much to read at the moment. I put them away in the house for us to look at and decide upon at some later date. One odd feature of the day was finding lots of cash, stashed in wallets or envelopes in drawers, pockets of bags, pockets of clothes. Most of this was in the last year or two, I think, as Mum became more and more nervous about not knowing where her cash was, so when she took some out she would stash it somewhere she would remember, then forgot, and so it went on.

—

At the end of our day taking stock, I carried the radio - still playing - to the front door as we left. It had kept at bay the house's unbearable silence, like a torch against darkness, until we stepped outside and shut the door behind us.

—

One of the first lessons you learn if you record sound is that no two forms of radio silence are the same. If you record an interview or an event, then you try to edit later, your most effective means of making those edits smooth is to use recorded silence from the same location, taken at the same time, to fill in the gap where the words have been removed. Try to use silence recorded in another location, or on a different day with subtly different background noise (air-con in the next room, winds outside, more bodies in the space) and the edit will jump out at the listener. So every radio producer is taught to end an interview or the recording of an event with the taking of what's called atmos, or wildtrack. During this time, usually around a minute, no-one must speak, or rustle their papers, or creak on the legs of their chair. So the producer holds up a microphone, and everyone looks down for a minute while the silence is recorded. It's a strange, rather wonderful way of ending a radio interview, like a shared moment of prayer or meditation. Again, to sit in a room where 'atmos' is being taken is to experience silence as attention.

—

In Alfred Lord Tennyson's Arthurian poem *Idylls of the King*, there is no shortage of noise and clamour – huge battles are fought, oaths are sworn, songs are sung and stories told. There are tournaments between knights, attended by rowdy courtiers, and banquets with hushed conversations in the wings. This was all grist to my mill when I was commissioned to adapt the *Idylls* for a radio drama. The vast scale and cast of Tennyson's poem did not make this an easy task, and I had to cut whole chapters, as well as making multiple edits within those that remained. But in its substance, if not in its scale, I found Tennyson's *Idylls* so suited to radio it could have been written specially for it, although when Tennyson wrote it, Marconi was still experimenting.

Tennyson knew not only how to use sound to dramatic effect, but crucially, how to use silence. As well as the small but significant silences he works into conversations within the tortured love triangle of Arthur, Lancelot and Guinevere, the poet uses two great silences almost as bookends to this cacophonous epic. The first, which comes at the end of Arthur's battle against the beasts and warlords who had brought his kingdom to its knees, is called into being by a shout from the king: '"Ho! they yield!" / So like a painted battle the war stood / Silenced, the living quiet as the dead, / And in the heart of Arthur joy was lord.'

'Like a painted battle the war stood' . . . On radio, a penetrating silence like this can be an intense moment of drama, as a medium known for constant speech and music breaks into active silence. 'Active' because this is a different silence from the silence of a radio unplugged. This is a silence made active by the powerful network of transmitters and receivers, all working at full power to bring – silence. It takes a lot of effort. This active silence has something of Simone Weil's 'attention'. And it is no accident that silences on radio often come before, after, or during poems or music.

—

Julia Margaret Cameron, who produced those unsettling early photographic images of the wise and foolish bridesmaids preparing (or failing to prepare) for the end of time, made a series to illustrate her friend Tennyson's Arthurian epic. Her series evokes scenes and characters from the poem, in full theatrical costume and with subtle, shadowy mysterious backgrounds. In one image of Merlin (played by the photographer's husband Henry) under the spell of Vivien, the trunk of a hollow oak was brought from the poet's garden as part of the backdrop. To a contemporary eye, there is a deep stillness to these scenes, though one of their most striking characteristics is Cameron's use of the slightest motion to create a ghosting effect.

There is a deep silence to them too, as in Tarkovsky's Polaroids. His prints capture the look of a real silence – often with an isolated static figure or none. Whether staged or not, they appear to capture a moment of stillness he chanced upon. In Cameron's images, the stillness and silence is foregrounded, contrived. She creates a mannered silence in *tableaux vivants*. Despite the set-dressing and costumes, her scenes from *Idylls of the King* are not a form of frozen time, they seem as unacquainted with chronology as the figures in religious icons, their faces utterly expressionless, inviting the viewer to look through them, not at them. Cameron's *Idylls* images are secular icons, a painted battle with a monochrome palette.

—

At the end of Tennyson's *Idylls of the King* there is a second massive hush. This time, he prefaces it with vivid descriptions of the final battle:

> And ever and anon with host to host
> Shocks, and the splintering spear, the hard mail hewn,
> Shield-breakings, and the clash of brands, the crash
> Of battleaxes on shatter'd helms, and shrieks
> After the Christ, of those who falling down
> Look'd up for heaven, and only saw the mist;
> And shouts of heathen and the traitor knights,
> Oaths, insult, filth, and monstrous blasphemies,
> Sweat, writhings, anguish, labouring of the lungs
> In that close mist, and cryings for the light,
> Moans of the dying, and voices of the dead.

This is not 'a painted battle', as Tennyson described the first silence in the *Idylls*. This is a real and vivid battle, and out of it, another silence emerges:

> Last, as by some one deathbed after wail
> Of suffering, silence follows, or thro' death
> Or deathlike swoon, thus over all that shore,
> Save for some whisper of the seething seas,
> A dead hush fell.

This time, Tennyson makes explicit the link between silence and death. And of course, that is the one place we can all expect to find deep silence. The elegy as a form can be – in part – an attempt at a kind of mysticism. How else would you describe the conjuring of the voices of the dead?

—

This all presupposes that there is such a thing as silence in the first place. John Cage, the radical composer famous for his so-called 'silent' music, in a piece called *4'33"*, is often misrepresented as a celebrant of silence. In fact, in a lecture published in 1961 he makes clear that: 'There is no such thing as an empty space or an empty time. There is always something to see, something to hear.' To test his unbelief in silence, Cage spent some time locked in an anechoic chamber at Harvard University. This is a space designed and built to eliminate all possibility of sound or echo. But as Cage sat in the chamber he heard the sounds of his own body, his nervous system, the flow of his blood.

4'33" is often referred to as *Silence*, but the first indication of Cage's idea for the piece came several years before in a planned piece under the title *Silent Prayer*. Cage, like Messiaen, was deeply concerned with the relationship between music and the spirit, and like Messiaen's musical exploration of eternity in the *Quartet*, his *4'33"* is a mystical act. Peace, like silence, is supposed to be an essential and fugitive state, something we've lost and should seek out. It's good for us. But speak to anyone in a monastic community, those expert wranglers of silence, and they say that their perceived withdrawal is anything but. Far from tranquil, their silent life is a confrontation with the self and the world, rather than a turning away. Like John Cage in the anechoic chamber they face fear and the self.

—

The final leg of sorting through my parents' house. Early start. Long day. Half each of the letters between Mum and Dad before they got married, half each of their diaries, half each of the letters between Dad and his parents and friends when he was on national service in Egypt, and so on with old photographs, autograph books et al. We finished with the garage and the garden shed, then packed our cars with boxes of things we don't have the strength or will to decide upon. But the skip is full again. Three large skips, and by the end almost everything went in. My sister said that when we first started to open cupboards and look in drawers – back in the autumn – she felt it was still their house and their things still carried something of them. But today she said she felt they were both now 'very far away'. I think that's right. They don't care about the house any more. We just need it to be cleared and handed on to the next owners.

The house-clearance vans arrive to finish the job. They swarm from room to room and make snap judgements, putting all the stuff for a 'general auction' into one van, and all the stuff for landfill in the other. They charge by the hour and work fast. By the time they're finished it's just bare walls and carpets. Six hours of solid work by four men with three vans, shuttling to and from the saleroom and the tip, and it's done. By late afternoon the vans have gone. I shut all the windows of the empty house, have one last look in each room and take some photographs, lock the front door for the final time and post my key back through the letter box. And that's it. It's been preying on our minds more than we knew – how today would go – so at least it's done now. The house without them in it was no longer theirs, however strong the memories and traces. It did take on though, in recent months as we went through all their stuff, the must and earnestness of a mausoleum, a tenuous kind of memorial holding them here, a place where they might still be met. So leaving it felt like a loss again. But it's someone else's house now, and so it has to be.

—

I kept trying to write a poem about elevens, starting with a number, seeing what might spin out of it. I really like that way of working, keeping the process open, seeing where the poem wants to go. But every new section I began to write seemed to close in on images of atrophy, of loss, of woundedness and the kind of pointless counting, the reckoning up, I was doing on the night of Mum's death. Emily Howard was going to set this poem for voices. The deadline for her work to start was looming. It was the beginning of winter. Three months on. My sister and I had been clearing the house on every spare weekend day, starting out picking through every drawer and putting things in boxes of things we should keep (loads), things we should discuss properly whether to keep (even more) and things we should give or throw away (hardly anything). By autumn we were filling skips on the drive.

There were aspects of the poem that were still rooted in the numbers – it was in eleven sections, and they could be read out of sequence (save the last two) so Emily could set them in loops if she wanted to, plus there was a half-hidden count with numbers running from eleven to one in reverse through each of the sections. But despite all that it was far from abstract. It had turned into an elegy for Mum. It was only when I acknowledged that inevitability that it began to come together. The title too, contained a nod to the number eleven, and to its internal loops. It also felt like a pair with the title of Dad's elegy. His was called 'Episodics'. Hers was called 'Elliptics'.

—

ELLIPTICS

I.M. IR

I

Full-tilt towards infinity, eleven hounds
track the earth's sharp curvature.
No bobtail pelt of hare,
no halt of wounded deer,
not in pursuit, just muzzle down and go
as the world turns towards them.
Dusk that never blossoms.
Endless vespers.

2

Night-long drive.
The road one step ahead.
Picture flowers by your bed:
deca-petalled heartleaf arnica,
child's drawing of a sun, full butter, sweetcorn,
wake up to a morning curtains cannot hold,
world out there for which
we have no words.

3

Houses dark and steep, oblivious –
their street numbers and names
half-lit on gates *three*, *five*, *seven*, *nine* –
now run out into fields.
Love alone brooks resurrection,
nothing else withstands its blaze,
a lock that picks itself.

4

Under our feet, below the sewers,
held by ligaments of a nameless stream,
a doctor-fish heals itself.
Scarred tench stutters into heartbeats,
ons and offs, ones and zeros, hum.
After winter's stasis,
this is life as bulb on the blink,

burnt-out filament,
arcing from silt to float downstream.
Now you become a shoal of *four*, *six*, *eight*,
and how salt, how singular,
how like the sea you are.

5

Seven swans in grief alight
on seven highways,
mistaking them for rivers,
cars schooling and shoaling,
pedestrians as trees weep on the banks,
blue lights scale the undersides of bridges.

6

Wildfires on the bare hills.
Three blackbird pairs on startle in their gardens.

7

Like a bird that has hit glass.
Like a rinsed-through,
freeze-dried version of yourself.
Like a loose suit of you
that nobody checked if you wanted to wear.
The wire-wool of your hair.
Pipe-cleaner fingers in a glove of skin.
Not knowing what realm you're in.

8

Be quiet, you say.
Beyond these walls is so much silence.
Damned if I can hear it.

9

On the way,
I reckoned up trios of street lamps
so as not to be outfaced by multiples.
Every time I thought of you
I lost my thread
and had to start again.

10

Rooks wake, warn and clatter.
Bees like loose wires under roof tiles.
The long-gone and the not-yet-here have better
things to do than pay attention to this room
but if they did they would

11

know this as the punctum
where love can be undone or done,
can be undone or done.

CHAPTER 7

Tangle of Rainbows for the Angel who Announces the End of Time

After the fury, the ecstasy. I've always loved the way the *Quartet* segues, with the briefest of pauses, from the furious dance in the sixth movement to the tangle of rainbows in the seventh. The furious dance ends with seven strident notes from the ensemble, to evoke the seven trumpets. The last 'trumpet blast' – the one that calls the end of time – is held, and held, and held until you think the clarinettist will run out of breath . . . then cut. A silence. Then comes the reward for all that 'terrible fortissimo', the granite and ice.

Messiaen's notes for his seventh movement go from straightforward information (informing the listener that some themes from section two return here) to pictures from Revelation (the mighty angel is back, but this time we focus on his rainbow crown) to an account of his dream-life: 'I hear chords and melodies, I see colours and forms; then I move beyond reality into ecstasy, dizziness, a whirl of interwoven superhuman sounds and colours. Swords of fire, flows of blue-orange lava, sudden stars; this is the tangle of rainbows.' His synaesthesia was magnified by the conditions in the labour camp, in particular the meagre rations, so his dreams became Technicolor visions. These visions drew him back to read the Book of Revelation, and he saw that in full colour too.

That's a powerful story, not least because of the musical riches he draws from the camp's privations. But his accounts of the visions remind me why I don't keep a dream diary. Are they useful to the dreamer alone? Or not even to the dreamer? Perhaps it's different if you're a composer yourself. Emily Howard tells me that Messiaen 'explains what he's doing with such clarity. It's incredible how clear to me this is.' I admire these explanatory notes as insights into the composer's intentions, but I wonder who they are actually for – fellow composers and musicologists, or players preparing to perform the piece, or listeners like me? Kate Romano finds them less helpful when reproduced in programme notes at *Quartet* concerts: 'It seems as if they are telling listeners what to feel.'

For me, most of Messiaen's notes sit apart from the music. I read them as a set of curiosities like abstract poems that I never call to mind when listening to the *Quartet*. The music makes its own pictures, its own poetry. There are moments, though, when the word he uses concurs perfectly with my changing experience as a listener. I used to love the dance of fury. Still do. But the wild wheeling and gyrating of the seventh section – 'Fouillis d'arcs-en-ciel, pour l'Ange qui annonce la fin du temps' – now sounds to me like a kind of ecstasy or, as Anthony Pople puts it 'a synaesthetic overwhelming of the senses'.

—

At the National Portrait Gallery's exhibition of portraits by the photographer William Eggleston, I found myself standing for longest in front of one of his best-known pictures, commonly known as *Marcia Hare in Memphis, Tennessee* taken in 1975. It's a famous image, of a young woman in a floral dress, lying back on a lawn with her arms outstretched either side of her, a camera loosely held in one hand. But through Eggleston's lens, that simple scene is transformed. He used techniques – in particular a process known as 'dye transfer' previously associated with commercial photography – to create a hyper-vivid image, so the greens and browns of the burnt-out grass are as intense as the copper of the woman's hair and the rosehip richness of the flowers on her dress. It is, as Tarkovsky saw his Polaroids, a solid object snatched from time. But the print it makes is so intense, so heightened. The woman in the picture is not just 'at peace', she's in reverie. One *Guardian* piece reports the photographer's personal title for the image, according to his son, as *Marcia whacked out on Quaaludes*.

—

My abstract poem on 'eleven' was hijacked, or hijacked itself, by an elegy. 'Elliptics' had been set by Emily and performed. The following summer I was walking along a clifftop, looking down from the path at the blinding sea below, swimmers in their own natural harbours, wet dogs beachcombing nose first in seaweed. Black spaniel ball-chasing. Pocket fishing boats beyond. Serious heat, for a shade-lover like me. I'm on a three-hour break between my events at a book festival in Guernsey. My first trip here, so I've cadged a lift to the far end of a cliff path to walk back to St Peter Port along the coast. I take off my jacket, and as I'm one arm in, one out, I get a sudden sense that this is a significant day. I can't work it out. I don't memorise dates. Can barely recall today's. Is it a birthday? I know it wasn't the date Dad went, nor Mum. I check my phone calendar. A year back. There it is, the last – though we didn't know it then – trip to see Mum in the care home. First anniversary of our final conversation. This is not an anniversary I want to keep, but somewhere in my head it has been kept. Her, returned to a fledgling, her reduced to that. Dropped in a cot. A curl, a kernel of herself. Her thinking she was in a hotel, but wondering why the bed was fenced. We didn't know the pandemic rules for this new care home. We knew we could visit once a week, no more. Masks. Lateral flow tests in the lobby, then back to the car park until the lines on the test resolved. One line and you're in. Two and you go home. We knew all this, but didn't ask about flowers. Were we allowed to take them? One less hoop to jump through, so no. We brought nothing but ourselves.

Now one year on all I can think is that we should have

taken flowers. There was one in 'Elliptics', but not one she loved and not a spray of them, no garland, no extravagance of tributes à la Milton's Lycidas. This is not an anniversary I want to keep. I take pictures on my phone of all the plants along the cliff path, to look them up later: sandgrass, pansy, hawkweed, bird's-eye, campion. I could be wrong about their names. She would know all of them. I wonder where she is, but wherever, I'm sure she neither knows nor cares about this floral roll call. Perhaps because she went before she went, a long, slow leaving from the present to the past and then beyond it, I have never cried about this loss. I can reason that, but nonetheless. And now a butterfly, a clumsy cabbage white above, beside, in front of me, drunk-dancing down the path. If it wasn't the truth, I'd leave it out. Too corny. On-the-nose. This day. This date. It is not an anniversary I want to keep.

When I came here, everyone said I must visit Hauteville House, the home of Victor Hugo in exile from France. I have been to a lot of dead and living writers' houses. But none like this. From local shops and flea markets, Hugo furnished the inside of his home to mirror the inside of his head. Room by room, it was peppered with odd, ornate touches to illustrate his personal passions, gripes and symbols. Tile-glazed walls with built-in niches for statues, carpeted ceilings, lush velvet swaggery in blood red, intricate wall mosaics of peacocks, carved mottos and charms, huge doors refashioned as tables, a 'terrible fortissimo' of patterns, colours and styles. He was not, it's fair to say, a minimalist when it came to interior design. I loved walking round the inside of his head. But one detail really struck me. On a bright, sea-facing window wall in the dining room is a tall dark-wood hooded chair positioned between two dazzling panes so it's impossible to see the detail without shading your eyes. This is Hugo's chair for his dead family and friends. The details include ornate gold and red painted carvings, initials and dates. Only the dead could sit there, a place reserved at all his dinners, a chance to meet all his guests, to be present even in their absence.

—

Sooner or later I had to come here. I've been picturing it for decades. Couldn't quite figure out why I should go, nor why I shouldn't. I have listened to the *Quartet* so many times without seeing Görlitz. Yet the story of its composition and premiere has become inseparable from the work itself. I hold fast to W. H. Auden's warning that 'no knowledge of raw ingredients' in a poet's life will explain the poems. But it hasn't stopped me travelling to the Audenhaus in Kirchstetten on the edge of the Vienna Woods to sit at the desk where he wrote so many of his late, great elegies and love lyrics.

In my first book of poems, most of them written when I was a student, the second poem is called 'Messiaen in Görlitz 1940'. I had planned to place it at the start of the book, but I was worried that a poem about the apocalyptic vision of a mystic modernist composer about the end of the world might not be a welcoming opener. For reasons now opaque to me, I tackled this issue by swapping it for a poem about an angel at a cement works. But that Messiaen poem was pivotal for me. I was in my early twenties when I wrote it. Writing about his metaphysics gave me a way to explore my own. But as the title 'Messiaen in Görlitz 1940' makes clear, my way into Messiaen's music was inseparable from that particular place and time. I set the poem the year before the January premiere, so the speaker in the poem is looking ahead to that event. Reading it now, it's a kind of prayer that closes with a wish that the end of time might actually come about during the premiere. The speaker is the composer himself, his voice: prophetic, inspired, devout. The *Quartet* had clearly unlocked something for me. I was smitten.

—

> I was born believing, able to see sounds as colours.
> The underfeeding in this camp has magnified that
>   faculty
> so birds spout northern lights, and guards shout
>   ribbons.

—

The town of Görlitz came through the Second World War architecturally intact, which is why it feels so familiar on this June afternoon. This is my first saunter through its historic sunlit squares and shady ginnels, but anyone who has sat through films like *The Grand Budapest Hotel*, *Inglourious Basterds*, *The Reader* or *The Book Thief* has been well rehearsed for it. The town's tourist information centre has a stand listing the numerous productions shot here. My two German friends only know it from the movies too. For Felix Sprang and Helga Schwalm, both from the former west, this is a long way east. Both are professors of English literature, and both are musical too. But it's fair to say they are Messiaen agnostics. It is a first visit here for all of us. We pass a busy cafe with tables outside. On the edge of the fray a man in a cream linen suit and homburg hat sips his coffee and looks up at us, then down to the thick hardback book he is reading. Film crew long gone, but he is still in character, marooned in the past. Life as method acting.

It has been a long morning. The stopping-train from Berlin Ostbahnhof has taken us through the lush Spreewald with its lacework of canals then on south-east for hours past halts with clutches of barns and farmhouses, small towns with new stations, vast flat expanses of fields and copses. As we left Berlin, Felix pointed out the parched trees at the trackside. He looks at trees a lot, wherever we go. Plants too. We went to Berlin's Treptower Park the previous day, on the trail of a Russian tank on a plinth. Felix remembered it from school trips to the east and was intrigued to see if it was draped in Ukrainian flags or daubed with slogans. I was mesmerised by the Soviet statuary and stone-carved quotations from Stalin. Felix looked at those too, but not with any more attention than he gave the trees around the perimeter. He has talked to me before about 'plant-blindness' – our tendency to see people, buildings, wide shots of landscapes, but to gloss over trees and plants as part of a backcloth to the interesting stuff. Countering this is necessary, he says, if we want to rebalance our relationship with the planet. I diagnose myself as plant-myopic. I don't know much flora by name, but as with the birdsong, I have an app on my phone which helps. Felix tells me he is dog-blind, as he can't recognise or name many breeds. This doesn't make me feel better. Maybe we are both tank-blind, because we couldn't find it. He wonders if his memory had misplaced it in the wrong part of the park, the wrong memorial.

—

The sprawl of Berlin is draining the water table and the plants and trees are drying up. But the further east and south we go, the greener it gets. In the Görlitz tourist information office, we are told that no taxi will take us over the river. The drivers don't want the complication of currency and permits. Görlitz is its own twin town. As borders were redrawn in 1945, this community – once centred on the River Neisse – was divided by it. The German film-set half of town is now a short bridge walk from its Polish alter ego, Zgorzelec. We are told that the best bet is to cross the border on foot, then to call a Polish taxi to take us to Stalag VIII-A.

—

> In the misery of this bitter bright Silesian December
> I long for an end to time, a finish to the mystery of God,
> the coarse-grained setting of faith into a blinding fact.

—

In 1941 when *Quatuor pour la fin du temps* received its premiere here, this camp held over 47,000 prisoners of war from across Europe. The taxi ride south was quicker than we expected. We are early so we stand in the empty car park reading an interpretation board with black-and-white images of prisoners. We can't see any remnant of the camp itself, just thick woodland and a path disappearing into it. At the edge of the car park, facing into the woods, stands a striking brick building split on the diagonal by a concrete set of steps to a roof terrace. It looks like a cut cake with the knife left in it.

 Twenty years ago there was no building here, no car park, no signage. Even local taxi drivers shook their heads if asked to be taken to Stalag VIII-A. This seventy-five-acre site on the outskirts of Zgorzelec was waste ground, a place of fly-tipping, dealers and feral dogs. It seemed that everyone on both sides of the river was content to see it reclaimed by the woods. It was Messiaen's *Quartet* that changed its fate when a German theatre director and musician – Albrecht Goetze – came across the score and noticed it was inscribed 'written in Stalag VIII-A in Görlitz, Silesia in January 1941'. Mesmerised by the music and the story of its making, Goetze travelled in autumn 2002 from his home in Munich to the site of the former Stalag. In later interviews, he recalled his shock at finding the site abandoned and forgotten, but declared that he wanted 'to spend my life and compose where such music was made'. He moved to Görlitz, worked as a music teacher and director to support himself, and teamed up with local historian Roman Złobicki who had been studying the story of the Stalag since the late 1960s. Through them, Meetingpoint Messiaen was created as an international centre for peace and reconciliation, to memorialise the stories and memories of prisoners of war and to celebrate the genesis here of this seminal work of visionary, modernist twentieth-century music. Now the European Centre for Memory, Education and Culture (the cut cake building) hosts a small permanent exhibition about the camp and the making of the *Quartet for the End of Time*, plus rehearsal and performance spaces with a focus on young people in particular. In conjunction with the cross-border Meetingpoint Messiaen – an office on either side of the river – they run International Messiaen Days and a performance of the *Quartet* here on the anniversary of the famous premiere – 15 January – every year.

—

> We have all felt the same last vital forces stirring,
> moving through the camp like water did before the pipes froze,
> the promise of all I have hoped for, have loved and still love.

—

In a side room off the main performance space, one wall is covered by interpretation boards with colour-coded aerial maps showing which barracks held the Soviet prisoners and which the Italians, French, British, Polish, Yugoslavians and Belgians. The Russian barracks are in red, on the edge of the camp. There are more of these than all the other colours put together. There are blown-up grainy pictures of prisoners and guards. One board holds a life-size composite of three Soviet POWs in mid-shot – chest to head – assembled like a medieval triptych with three shaved gaunt figures staring hard at us. Around their necks hang boards on string bearing the name of the camp and their individual prisoner numbers. It is not easy to meet their eyes, but to look away feels wrong too. The prisoner on the left looks familiar. Who was he? I scan the board. No name. Later the resemblance lands. It's Martin Keown – former Arsenal defender turned *Match of the Day* pundit. For obvious reasons I do not share this with the others.

Our two guides – Alexandra Grochowski and Klaudyna Michalska – tell us more about conditions in the Stalag. Alexandra tells us that diet and sanitation were poor and the work regime punishing. In accordance with their racial ideology, the German guards were selective in their brutality. For some – including many French, English and Anzac prisoners – there were the distractions of rugby games, concerts and amateur dramatics. There was a camp newspaper written and produced by French prisoners. But these concessions were not granted to the Soviet prisoners. Why were French prisoners like Messiaen, captured in Verdun, brought to a camp so far east? Because, says Alexandra, any attempt to flee for home would require not just an escape but a 500-mile trek after it.

We shuffle along to the board marked *Quatuor pour la fin du temps* and Alexandra hands us over to Klaudyna, herself a double-bassist, to take over the Messiaen part of the tour. This board has a background picture of a smiling Olivier Messiaen leaning on an upright piano with a boyish musician – hands on keys – looking over his shoulder down the lens. At the back of the shot, a violinist stands with a bow resting on the strings. He is wearing a heavy jumper tucked into thick, high-waisted trousers. The others are similarly dressed for the cold. Above these photographs is a montage featuring sample pages from the (to me) impenetrably complex score of the *Quartet*, a handwritten programme for the premiere dated 15 January 1941 and a page of tributes from the violinist, clarinettist and cellist thanking their pianist and composer for giving them the 'miracle' of this premiere, describing the experience as a voyage to 'a wonderful paradise' which lifted them out of 'this abominable earth'. Down the side of the board is a list of Messiaen's eight titles for the *Quartet*'s movements translated from the French into Polish, German and English. I'm momentarily distracted by the word '*Regenbogen*' and how hard it must be to write singable German songs about rainbows.

The last board is bare and simple, highlighting again the edge-of-site location of the Russian barracks, along with a note that – according to the camp authorities – the Geneva Convention did not apply to German relations with the USSR, so there was no protection for the Soviet POWs. A quoted report from a former Belgian prisoner at Stalag VIII-A said that Russian prisoners died daily of dysentery and typhus. They were so malnourished and sick that two bodies were put in each casket then taken by cart pulled by their fellow prisoners to the mass grave behind the camp. This was not a concentration camp. The prisoners here were forced labour, working in nearby warehouses, factories and farms. All interaction and conversation between locals and prisoners was strictly forbidden.

For a western prisoner like Messiaen, work and conditions were hard, but compared to the Soviet prisoners his was a privileged life in camp. Not every French or

Belgian POW survived Stalag VIII-A, as disease and fatigue and the violence of the guards took their toll, but most did. Not every Soviet POW died of illness or was worked to death or shot, but many were. Our guides tell us the camp was brutal, but Messiaen was already a noted young composer when he was brought here, and a music-loving German officer gave him a place to work plus paper and pencils. When he was captured, he had scores stashed in his bag. He was permitted to keep them. He was, we are told, even granted a request that his watch duty should coincide with dawn so he could listen and transcribe the birds.

    The guides leave us for ten minutes to look at the glass museum cases on the adjacent wall full of objects found or dug up on the site. This is just the backstory. After this break we will be led into the woods, to be shown the exact site of the stage set up in a washroom for the famous premiere. Felix, Helga and I look at the objects in silence. Already the story of Messiaen and the *Quartet for the End of Time* feels unmoored from this place. We were more struck by the fate of the Soviet prisoners. In the middle of the room is a model of the camp showing the layout of the grey barracks with their gently sloping roofs, the bright synthetic grass and the matchstick fence posts around the perimeter with a thumb-sized watchtower on each corner. None of this is making sense. At least not enough. Even the legend of the premiere, with its custom composition to suit the available clapped-out instruments, is fading on the page. Our guides say that eyewitness accounts confirm some instruments were bought new from the town of Görlitz for the premiere, and that the cello had its full complement of strings. I cannot yet connect it all. Maybe the woods will make more sense. We stare through glass at the lit shelves of relics. I find I'm counting them.

—

> Two large earthenware bottles, one medium, one small all without stoppers
> One rusted bolt
> Two rusted, holed helmets like barnacles
> One fat clear glass bottle prone on its side, cork-less, ship-less
> One lapis blue leather flask
> Three pipe bowls with no stems
> Seven assorted coins
> Seven stars from uniforms
> Forty-two tunic buttons
> Four military dog tags
> Two pin badges bright as fish eyes
> One key too big to lose
> One shield-shaped token with a cross on it
> One rust-blasted can marked 'powdered milk'.
> One spoon with 'F Carovillano' carved into the handle
> Two broken combs

—

The *Quartet* is an apocalyptic work. For the composer, that means it is eschatological – concerned with the 'last things' that would complete the Christian story from creation to redemption. It is apocalyptic too, in that it draws on the Book of Revelation, an apocalyptic text in the original sense of prophecy, of revealing what will happen, ultimately, to the relationship between God and humanity. But the *Quartet* is often seen as apocalyptic in the colloquial sense too, concerned with catastrophe and desolation. Its genesis story, the fact that it was completed and premiered here in Stalag VIII-A, means its apocalypse is seen through the narrow lens of a particular time and place – a Nazi labour camp in Europe at one of the darkest moments in twentieth-century history. But Messiaen's real focus, the driving force of the *Quartet*, comes after the apocalypse, after the end, when we are released from the abyss of time into eternity. It is, in that purest sense, a post-apocalyptic work of art.

Jakob Böhme, that other visionary resident of Görlitz, was also working at what felt like an apocalyptic moment, the brutal Thirty Years War in central Europe. Both Messiaen and Böhme attended to the mystery of God, exploring that mystery through their work and visions, and both were captivated by the promise of an end to that mystery where, as St Paul writes, we will no longer look 'through a glass darkly', but 'face-to-face'. Messiaen spoke of the *Quartet* (dedicated to the Angel of the Apocalypse) as an expression of his longing for a consummation of the mystery of God, for faith to reach its fulfilment in fact, in a face-to-face encounter with the Creator. In Böhme's writing, the essence of God – including all the energies and forces of creation – was expressed in the word salitter. Görlitz was a hotbed of alchemy in the seventeenth century, so salitter – with its link to the fertilising and explosive properties of saltpetre – was maybe not such an obscure image of God's essence.

When Cormac McCarthy used it in his post-apocalyptic novel *The Road*, it certainly was. It's just one line. The father, whose journey of survival with his young son following an unspecified global catastrophe is the 'road' of the title, stands in a silent street and is aware of 'the salitter drying from the earth'. What could that mean? It's not in the dictionary. The fact that McCarthy used a line from Böhme as an epigraph in his previous novel *Blood Meridian* – a typically gnomic Böhme phrase about the life of darkness – gave the nod to look in that direction for the source of 'salitter'. McCarthy's use of it is unsettling – the last of God, the essence of life and creation reduced to a slick, a puddle being burnt off by the sun. But saltpetre, in the old way, had to be leached and dried to come into its own. Is this an image of the death of God? Or the first sign of God's return?

—

It is a humid June day in Görlitz, midweek, mid-afternoon. The woods are full of life – not just the unseemly muscling-in of greenery but a cacophony of birdsong. Mosquitoes too, not a smog of them, just enough to keep us in a constant semaphore. We are the only walkers on the new-laid gravel path tracing the former main street through the former Stalag. The growth was cut back hard, to make space for the paths. 'The forest was much thicker then, with all the mosquitoes,' says Alexandra. 'It was quite horrible.' This is disputed ground. Part of it is earmarked for a new housing estate. Alexandra says they are fighting the plan as they don't want to be running memorial events when there's a barbecue party on the other side of the track. She thinks there may still be bodies in the ground here. The local people are divided. Some want it to remain as a memorial. Others argue that the city needs more homes and lacks space to build them. The guides are proud of their memorial building, but ongoing funding is tight and they are reliant on volunteers to keep the place going. The dream would be for the German and Polish governments to save the Stalag site and preserve it as a permanent memorial. The Messiaen connection has brought in a little money, but not much and music funders are focused more on performance than remembrance. 'There's nothing to see,' says Helga. And she's right. The invisibility of the Stalag is striking. To offset the absence, interpretation boards appear at key sites along the path, complete with blown-up photographs of the camp and individual prisoner stories. Beyond the boards, I can pick out the occasional moss-coated edge of a concrete block, but mostly it's a tangle of green, a rude fury of new growth. My imagination is failing me here.

We turn a corner and find a large, abstract metal sculpture. The plan is to commission eight of these, each a response to one of the sections of Messiaen's *Quartet*. Visitors will be able to listen on headphones to each section of the music while looking at the corresponding sculpture. Each piece is centred on a slim stainless-steel cross with a range of other metals shaped around it, intended to weather in over the years at different rates producing different forms and colours. This one has a metal wave emerging from the undergrowth on one side and disappearing into the other. I know it must be representing a sound wave or the flow of time, but all I can see is a huge flat silver snake, alarmed by our approach, about to disappear into one of the hidden tunnels. This one corresponds, we are told, to the fifth movement.

—

> A sympathetic guard brings pencils and manuscript.
> We can only make with what we have; in God I have
>   it all,
> but here a three-stringed cello, piano, violin and
>   clarinet.

—

We stop by a barracks, built for 150 prisoners but routinely housing 300. In the Soviet section it was 600. '*UWAGA! GLEBOKIE WYKOPY*' is printed on a small yellow sign nailed to a birch trunk. ATTENTION! DEEP EXCAVATIONS. But there is no trace of a barracks left here. After the war, local people used whatever they could salvage from the abandoned camp to build and repair their houses. All that remains is a large concrete square with a lid on it. This was the night toilet, Klaudyna tells us. Most of the relics in glass cases in the visitor centre came from here, along with 'four huge guns'. Anything the prisoners wanted to keep out of the way of the guards was thrown in here.

Archaeologists have worked on various parts of the camp, but the foundations of the barracks are hard to pick out. The dream, says Alexandra, would be to uncover all the foundations, have them properly studied by archaeologists then covered with glass to protect it from the weather and preserve it. We walk past the site of a kitchen block, where thousands of visitors were fed. One block for the Soviets, one for the rest. The diet was meagre – cold soup and a little horsemeat. No meat for the Soviets.

Our guides lead us down the path to the next stop in our tour. They are working so hard to bring this place to life, to keep it as a memorial. Their vision and belief in the importance of what happened here is evident, but funds are hard to come by. 'There's not enough music in the story to draw funding from musical foundations,' says Helga as we follow them down the path, 'and not enough left of the camp to attract the big educational foundations.' It must be very difficult. I ask about the birds in these woods. There is a lot of birdsong, so with Messiaen in mind I'm wondering what they are. Alexandra says a German ornithologist – Dr Markus Ritz, an ornithologist with the Senckenberg

Museum in Görlitz – spent time here and documented all the birds. And there were plenty.

—

Zilpzalp (chiffchaff), *Fitis* (willow warbler), *Rotkehlchen* (robin), *Mönchgrasmücke* (blackcap), *Star* (starling), *Kohlmeise* (great tit), *Gartengrasmücke* (garden warbler), *Singdrossel* (song thrush), *Amsel* (blackbird), *Kernbeißer* (hawfinch), *Goldammer* (yellowhammer), *Baumpieper* (tree pipit), *Blaumeise* (bluetit), *Eichelhäher* (jay), *Buntspecht* (great spotted woodpecker), *Schwanzmeise* (long-tailed tit), *Nachtigall* (nightingale), *Pirol* (oriole), *Buchfink* (chaffinch), *Zaunkönig* (wren), *Heckenbraunelle* (hedge sparrow), *Gartenbaumläufer* (treecreeper), *Sumpfmeise* (marsh tit), *Grauschnäpper* (spotted flycatcher), *Kranich* (crane), *Wendehals* (eurasian wryneck), *Neuntöter* (red-backed shrike), *Heidelerche* (woodlark), *Gimpel* (bullfinch), *Wespenbussard* (honey buzzard), *Waldlaubsänger* (wood warbler), *Dorngrasmücke* (whitethroat), *Schwarzspecht* (black woodpecker), *Stockente* (mallard), *Ringeltaube* (woodpigeon), *Weidenmeise* (willow tit), *Grünfink* (greenfinch).

This bird-choir will not be identical to the one that tutored the composer on his early morning watch. There are more trees now, closer and younger and denser, since the camp was demolished and the woods reclaimed it. But it's a good approximation. It is ridiculous, I know, since they are both so common, but when I saw the two avian stars of the *Quartet* – blackbird and nightingale – on Dr Ritz's list, it felt like a genetic link to Messiaen's music. Blackbirds and nightingales have wide repertoires, local accents, individual songs or variations. I like to think we heard some of the same songs on that afternoon in Görlitz that he heard in 1940, performed by the descendants of his choir.

—

Messiaen only began his *'cahiers de notations des chants d'oiseaux'* in the early 1950s. This series of notebooks is a remarkable record of his travels, his obsession with birdsong and his ability to map that birdsong onto particular locations. His descriptions of the wild places he visited (often when travelling overseas where his own music was performed) are as full of sounds and colours as his music. Over a decade before he developed the *cahiers* as part of his working practice, his notation of birdsong in Görlitz was more impressionistic, yet to be worked into a system. Nonetheless, musicologist Robert Sherlaw Johnson notes that despite the composer's use – at this point – of the word *'oiseau'* in the score, it's possible to pin that down – in 'Liturgie de cristal', the first movement specifically – to violin playing nightingale and clarinet playing blackbird. Although some ornithologists have argued that Messiaen's birds are difficult to identify from his music, the composer believed that birdsong was so virtuosic, so rapid, so high in register, so full of unplayable (by humans) microtonal shifts that he had to transpose it to be playable as music in our limited range.

—

> Its world premiere will take place in a washroom,
> where I know this French and Polish audience of peasants,
> doctors and priests will be the most attentive I have seen.

—

Our tour snakes round another few bends in the path. The mosquitoes are beginning to dominate. The woods are in rude health and the path feels provisional. Left untended, how long before the path would be invisible? A year? Six months? We stop at the next point in the tour and Klaudyna – the guide who is also a musician – joins Alexandra to tell us where we are. 'So here was the theatre barracks where there was the premiere and a lot of other events.' She gestures towards a densely overgrown patch of ground between tall, pillar-straight silver birches. We are at the edge of the former Stalag now. A runner lopes past outside the perimeter with a number on his back. 'The church barracks was next to it,' Alexandra adds. 'So you can see this is the middle of the barracks, because you have this washing part.' She points to a slab of concrete the size of a single bed. It has been semi-reclaimed by grass and moss but with a section of smooth slip-brown concrete exposed. 'So here were the people, the audience, in front of the washing things.' It is dawning on me now. 'So, that's where the stage was, where the players would have been?' Klaudyna nods.

That slab of concrete is all that's left of the stage in what was once a washroom-cum-theatre barracks. I stand and stare at it as the others walk on to the next stop on the tour. I take a photograph. Take a video, pointlessly, as there's barely a ripple in the grass and nobody else in frame. This is the exact location of the most celebrated, hallowed, mythologised musical premiere of the twentieth century. I wish I had time to stand here with my headphones on and listen to *Quatuor pour la fin du temps*. There is a frisson about this spot. I can't deny it. There is something here. It seems right that there is no interpretation board or a path right up to where they played that day. It is not marked nor hallowed here. Without the guides with us there would be no way of knowing where the premiere took place.

—

The end of the seventh movement surprises me every time. A shimmering heat haze, like a desert road that won't hold still under the sun as it shrugs off its skin. Then a punchline as perfect and incongruous as a kazoo or a swannee whistle, only on the clarinet – five shrill shrieks – then the sound of a piano falling downstairs.

—

I catch up with our guides and ask more questions. They gently start to complicate the story of the premiere. I received that famous story when I first heard the music, and have repeated it to others over the years. That version, no doubt twisted and turned in multiple retellings, holds this music as a cry of hope and longing to be liberated from the labour camp, a stand against war and suffering, a witness to faith and the human spirit. It was written for the only four instruments available in the camp with prisoners able to play them – a three-stringed cello, a beaten upright piano with sticky keys, a violin and a clarinet. Out of this makeshift set-up came a first performance so entrancing that an audience of thousands crammed into a washroom barracks to hear it on a freezing January night, with sick and injured prisoners laid out at the front. It is up there with the story of Stravinsky's explosive premiere of *Rite of Spring* in Paris as a legend of twentieth-century music. Except it doesn't quite stand up.

My understanding of the story was changed largely by the musicologist Rebecca Rischin's forensic retelling of it, based on detailed interviews with players and audience members. Rischin and other scholars and lovers of Messiaen's music have shown that the audience was much smaller than the story suggests, perhaps a few hundred at most. Though nutrition and sanitation were poor, sickness rife and living conditions certainly grim, there were nonetheless – for French and English prisoners at least – regular theatre events, sports competitions, concerts and a camp newspaper produced by and for the prisoners. The already celebrated composer was given duties in the camp library, time to work on his music, and the wherewithal to write it down. As our Görlitz guides confirm, the upright piano at the premiere – though hardly concert standard – was playable and had been brought into the camp to help with Messiaen's work. The three-stringed battered cello had all four strings and was purchased from the town of Görlitz specially for the performance. The clarinet was brought into the camp by the accomplished musician who played it at the premiere. Three of the eight movements were largely written before Messiaen arrived in Görlitz, with one more written in the camp before he conceived of the *Quartet*. Although some prisoners on that January night of the premiere were transfixed by the music's visionary beauty, others found it too atonal and hated it.

None of this matters. At least, not to me. On the making of *Quatuor pour la fin du temps* – its sources, its visions, its intent – Messiaen was clear and consistent from the start. Its key source was the Book of Revelation, a part of the Bible some believers skirt around and others employ as an apocalyptic field guide. For Messiaen, Revelation was a work of wonder and enchantment, a promise of fulfilment in the eternal presence of God. He denied that the apocalyptic references in *Quartet* were references to the camp or the fate of its prisoners, insisting that as he was writing it, he was so absorbed in his visions of the end of time that of all the soldiers held in Stalag VIII-A he was 'probably the only one who was free'.

—

> Though it is not for us to know or guess, perhaps as we begin
> to play the eighth and final movement – beyond the day of rest
> after creation into ceaseless light and peace –
>
> the end may come, the seventh angel crowned with a rainbow,
> one foot in flames on the Pacific Ocean, the other
> burning without melting, light as a leaf on Silesian snow.

—

We are offered a choice of ending the tour at the memorial by the main building to pay our respects there, or at the camp cemetery. I look at Felix and Helga. They both say it's up to me. In the years when Stalag VIII-A was forgotten, one part of the site was still tended. Now the camp cemetery will be the last stop on our walk.

After ten minutes' walk along the track through the woods, overtaken by cyclists going full pelt down the woodland paths, we arrive at a metal gate. This is not like any war cemetery I have seen. There are no headstones for a start. No paths to let visitors walk up and down the rows and lay flowers at particular graves. It is a flat grass rectangle the size of a suburban house and garden, marked out from the wasteland around it by a wall topped with decorative coping like piped icing. The ground is ribbed, as if to suggest individual graves, but a sign in Polish, German, English and Russian suggests otherwise: 'About 10,000 Soviet prisoners of war lost their lives at the Stalag VIII-A and are buried at this site.' It is a mass grave. There are no names. It is possible, we are told, that there are other mass graves around the edges of the camp.

An optional lantern with a large candle is provided. We say yes and our guide lights the candle with a plastic lighter, holding out the lantern to the three of us. Helga and Felix nod to me and stand back. I am the one who wanted to come here, who wanted to see where *Quartet for the End of Time* was written and premiered. But this feels miles from Messiaen, the visitor centre, the sculptures and the history tour. I have been recording the tour as we go round, partly so I wouldn't forget anything, but partly because – as Seán Street says – it will give me an immersive record of this visit. I can't go up to the memorial with a lantern in one hand and a sound recorder in the other. It wouldn't be right. There's nowhere to put it down, so I hand the recorder to Felix while I take the lantern and climb the few steps to place it among the flowers, cards and candles. I stand back and start to cross myself, then stop and bow my head instead. I walk back down and notice that Felix is alongside me, holding the recorder low to catch the sound of my shoes on the steps. Of course. He thought I wanted him to keep recording.

>Where once stood Stalag VIII-A now stand:
>Silver Poplar
>Cherry
>Mountain Ash
>Birch
>Maple
>Hornbeam
>Linden
>Beech
>Hawthorn
>Young oak
>Older oaks (at the cemetery)

Felix emails me, the day after the Görlitz tour: I woke up this morning feeling that Stalag VIII-A is a paradoxical place: nature reclaiming the area with such peaceful vivacity plus the photographs of happy POWs playing football, basketball, 'enjoying' a cultural life including the *Quartet for the End of Time*. As I said on the train, I have been to extinction camps like Auschwitz, Buchenwald, Neuengamme, Dachau and concentration camps like Esterwegen – and I couldn't/can't help comparing the feel of visiting Stalag VIII-A with those visits. So my empathy/sympathy gravitated towards the Soviet prisoners. These are conflicted emotions and thoughts. I am sure all this will work on me for a while.

So I reply: I've been thinking about Görlitz a lot too. And I've reached the same conclusion, that it was a strange and conflicted place. The fate of the Soviet prisoners was appalling, but the French prisoners like Messiaen seemed to live in relative privilege, though they also suffered hardship and privation. I was glad to have visited, since the genesis narrative of the *Quartet for the End of Time*, which is such an iconic piece of twentieth-century music, has become legendary. So if you're writing about the *Quartet*, you have to go there. Having gone there, however, I ended up feeling that the place had almost nothing to do with the music. Sure, the premiere took place there, but the music – by the composer's own admission – was not intended as a response to captivity, the camp or their living conditions. Messiaen never went back to Görlitz after the war.

—

My sense of Messiaen is that his development as a composer was driven by his idiosyncratic musical and theological vision, and if he hadn't been in the camp he might have written something very much like the *Quartet* in Paris, or Verdun, or wherever. I wondered if our guides may have felt this too. It's a complicated story, teasing out the relationship between the camp and the *Quartet*. I felt that the music was both an attraction and a distraction. It is the reason people like me come to Görlitz, the reason people all over the world know the name of the town having read it on concert programmes or the back of old CDs or the write-ups on Spotify or wherever this *Quartet* is mentioned. But I came away thinking the real life of the place now comes through its work with young people from across the world. Its title is 'European Centre for Memory, Education and Culture'. Every summer, groups of young people come to work here, 'to experience history and work together peacefully at an authentic historical site, which has been a place of despair and death for many'.

—

On the long train ride back to Berlin, the three of us are silent. I'm listening to my audiobook of *Metaphysical Animals* again. It's a brilliant work, insightful and anecdotal, but my head is full of Messiaen and Görlitz and the site of Stalag VIII-A, so as my gaze drifts out of the window to the darkening horizon and back, my mind drifts too, and I keep having to rewind to catch something I missed.

Then, a sudden radiant detail. The year after the Görlitz premiere, Murdoch and Midgley, newly graduated and travelling from Oxford to London for the first time since the

Blitz, emerged from Marylebone Station's bomb-damaged exit to be 'greeted by an abundance of butterflies. So many of the city's birds had been driven away by the Blitz, joining the one million child evacuees in the surrounding countryside, that the capital now suffered plagues of caterpillars through the silent springs, followed by butterfly-filled summers.' I scroll back to listen again. What a vision. Apocalyptic in its beauty born of horror. I imagine what Messiaen might think, a metaphysical animal for sure, if he arrived in a city to see clouds of fragile colours but without a note of birdsong. 'Silent Spring', Rachel Carson's prescient foretelling of environmental loss in the 1950s, now looks more bleakly true than ever, as bird populations fall and their songs fade out. For all the traditional imagery of 'the end' as a cacophony of thunder, trumpets, mighty voices, this would be a slow and steady fade down to a whimper, then to nothing.

—

Seán Street told me the story of a sound recording, made in the 1980s, of the Kaua'i 'ō'ō bird – a honeyeater – in the forests of Hawaii. 'It was the last of its species, calling to its mate, but its mate had already died. So this bird in the recording is calling out into a silent universe waiting for a voice to come back, but it never does, and never can again.'

—

Is it the story of the *Quartet*'s premiere that gives its title such an undertow? If ever I mention it to someone who doesn't know the piece, the title alone suggests a bleak and heavy listen. If they've come across the Görlitz story then it sounds like a daunting prospect, one to put on a list for the future, like a harrowing film you think you should watch but never quite makes it to the top of your list. Messiaen would be surprised and disappointed. He wasn't interested in apocalyptic dread and destruction. 'I did not in any sense want to comment upon the Apocalypse,' he said. 'My only wish was to articulate my desire for the dissolution of time.' And he articulates that desire, and its fulfilment, throughout the *Quartet*, reaching its culmination in the eighth section reaching beyond the end of time. Anthony Pople points out that the final movement is marked *'extrêmement lent'* (exceedingly slow) explaining that this is a term 'which Messiaen associates with a state of ecstasy'.

—

SEVEN DENOUEMENTS

(i)

Back from the lost, the one you miss the most
is at the door: *I've given up the ghost.*

TANGLE OF RAINBOWS

(ii)

Old bells croak into voice to mark the hour,
a carillon of doves breaks from the tower.

(iii)

Gutters, grids and downpipes overflow.
You stand and soak, forgetting all you know.

(iv)

That song so sure you hardly dare begin
– you sing it, and an orchestra joins in.

(v)

A coin-toss: to set out again, or stay?
You snatch it from the air and walk away.

(vi)

All those feints, false trails, cross-purposes.
At last you catch yourselves off-guard and kiss.

(vii)

A blade cuts through the ropes – you are undone,
you kick the chair across the room and run.

CHAPTER 8

Praise to the Immortality of Jesus

Beyond the end of time. We have crossed the river. 'Louange à l'Immortalité de Jésus' ('Praise to the Immortality of Jesus') is the final piece of the *Quartet*. But this eighth movement is not about incense and ether. Messiaen's notes anchor it to the body, to the Word made flesh and the resurrection of the body. This movement is paired with the fifth, both written before Görlitz and united by the word '*louange*', meaning praise or eulogy. The fifth is in praise of the '*éternité*' of Jesus and the eighth in praise of his '*immortalité*'. The composer's notes for this final movement are his familiar heady blend of musical specifics (its big violin solo echoes the big cello solo in the fifth movement), and theological explanation, but the central focus of these two '*louanges*' is Jesus as God – in the fifth – and Jesus as man in the eighth.

The ascent of – as Messiaen has it – the child towards the father, of 'the deified creature towards Paradise' is one of the glories of the *Quartet*. The four players are pared back to piano and violin in this last section. The piano is

PRAISE TO THE IMMORTALITY OF JESUS

minimal, meditative, a subtle heartbeat as the violin begins what Anthony Pople calls its 'slow, weaving ascent'. It is the sound of eternity, beyond time, beyond struggle, beyond the apocalypse. It is all love.

—

I once visited an eminent music critic I had come to know, in his final days in a care-home cot, barely able to communicate. His friends were playing him pieces of music they knew he had cherished, but he couldn't bear them now, shouting, 'Take it off, I hate it!' I remember thinking this was a sign of the level of his loss, that even his favourite music had become unlistenable to him. But one of his oldest friends, himself a musician, was not so sure. 'We might just be playing him the wrong recordings.' I remembered this when I was listening to two versions of the *Quartet*'s final movement. Yet again, comparing my two chosen recordings – one from 1956 (with Messiaen himself playing) and one from 2000 – there's a stark difference. It's fair to say here that I'm unlikely to be a guest on Radio 3's *Record Review*, where experts judge one recording of a seminal work to be definitive and another unlistenable. As a rule, they sound identical to me. So I'm aware that there are levels of listening. In non-classical music, I have a nerdy knowledge of cover versions, can tell you which is best and why. With classical pieces, I tend to pick the first version on the streaming list. Except with the *Quartet*.

'*Extrêmement lent*'. That's the composer's instruction to players for this radiant final movement. As if that nod to ecstasy isn't clear enough, he adds 'it is all love'. As long as you play the right notes, I reckon it's impossible to knock the beauty out of this movement. It's one of the most perfect pieces I know. But the ecstasy is so magnified in the more recent version, I find the composer's own recording hard to bear now. In 1956 it took the players just under seven and a half minutes to play this final eulogy to eternal love. In 2000 it took nearly two minutes longer and sounds – to this listener – far closer to the composer's vision than his own recording half a century before.

I could be wrong. That 1956 recording had Messiaen himself as performer and guide. But then I know from poetry that the voice of the poet is not the same as the voice, or voices, in their poems. I'm interested to hear the poet's own performance of a poem, but that doesn't make it definitive. Some poets are remarkable readers, but you don't have to go to many poetry readings to realise that the best performance of a poem might come from somebody else. I would be fascinated to hear a recording of Emily Dickinson's 'Because I could not stop for death' or John Donne reading 'Death be not proud', not least to hear how they interpreted the music of their own work. But they might be awful. Even if they were wonderful readers (though very different as I suspect those two would be) that wouldn't make their readings definitive, nor even necessarily the best.

—

PRAISE TO THE IMMORTALITY OF JESUS

A month after the premiere, Messiaen had left Stalag VIII-A and was on his way home to Paris. He hadn't tried to escape from the camp when others did, as he believed it was God's will that he should be there. It's not entirely clear why or how he was released. There's a suggestion that his former teacher Marcel Dupré may have had some influence, but so did his already rising reputation as a composer. Rebecca Rischin suggests that the composer was released along with other *soldats musiciens*: 'men who had been drafted to serve in the armed forces as musicians' but did not carry arms. On his return home, Messiaen was emaciated and weak, with swollen fingers, his hands deformed by chilblains. But by May he was teaching at the Paris Conservatoire and composing again. There was a French premiere of *Quatuor pour la fin du temps* in Paris, which garnered mixed critical reactions, including some discomfort with its composer's extravagantly faith-fuelled notes on his inspiration and intentions for the music.

In the months and years that followed, Messiaen's music was performed more and more, but the *Quartet* was slow to catch up. When events were held to commemorate the war effort, with music by French composers written in captivity or under occupation, the *Quartet* was often excluded. Rischin suggests that this was less a conservative response to the music's revolutionary modernism and more an objection to its focus – visions of Revelation rather than the suffering and struggles of soldiers. Yet ironically, as Rischin points out, it was Messiaen's *Quartet* that would become universally identified with the suffering of prisoners of war: 'It would be the *Quartet* alone that would stand the test of time.' This focus on the eschatological future was unwavering for Messiaen. According to Peter Hill and Nigel Simeone, nearly two decades later in the early 1960s he was resisting the traditional role of music as a solemn elegy or memorial. Commissioned to compose a sacred work 'to the glory of the dead of two world wars', Messiaen's acceptance came with a note that *Et Expecto Resurrectum* would be 'a work for an orchestra of brass instruments, concerning the Resurrection of the Dead'.

He went on to be one of the twentieth century's most celebrated composers. His wife Clare died after a long illness in 1959, and he later married his long-standing musical collaborator and former pupil, the pianist Yvonne Loriod. With Loriod, he became one of the century's most fervent birdsong recordists, filling *cahier* after *cahier* with transcriptions and notations, while his wife made audio recordings as a backup. The birdsongs he incorporated for the first time in *Quartet* grew more and more central to his work, culminating in the audio equivalents of mass murmurations in which birdsongs sweep and interweave, rise and fall in wildly ambitious pieces like *Catalogue d'oiseaux* and *La Transfiguration de Notre Seigneur Jésus-Christ*. The Messiaens even made an excursion to New Caledonia to catch the song of the rare gerygone – chosen by the composer as the voice of an angel for his opera about St Francis of Assisi.

—

This is ordinary. Not just ordinary, it is right. Everybody should live to bury (or burn, or drown, though these both sound more brutal) the remains of their parents. It is the order of things. The whole line then shifts one step forward towards the cliff edge. For many, of course, the order is broken. But if you're lucky, this is how it's meant to go. Our parents both reached their eighties, albeit with some scares along the way. They outlived their own parents, met their grandchildren. But none of this has stopped us dreading this bright September afternoon in Coniston. At the end of her memoir on her mother's death, Simone de Beauvoir concludes: 'There is no such thing as a natural death: nothing that happens to a man is ever natural, since his presence calls the world into question. All men must die: but for every man his death is an accident and, even if he knows it and consents to it, an unjustifiable violation.'

The Lake District was an important place for them. Like of lot of Lancastrians, they had known it from childhood (Mum was evacuated there to escape the bombing of Salford docks), from school trips, stags and hens, holidays with us when we were kids. They even went there for their honeymoon. So it's fitting to bring them back here, albeit in two water-soluble urns in the boot of my sister's car. 'I've been wondering if this is the right thing,' she says. Mum never learnt to swim, she was worried about deep water. We sit for a coffee at the lakeside and talk about it. Nothing seems obvious. Should we bury the ashes somewhere with a stone, a place to visit? They were adamant, in later life, that they didn't want that. They hated the idea that we would feel we had to go somewhere to tend a plot or dress and redress it with flowers. None of their parents has a marked plot. And Coniston Water is a place to visit, a place to honour them. Today with the low sun and dark clouds putting on a shadow play, with us – dog-walkers, cafe-goers, boat-trippers – cast as players, it felt as if the stage was set. Besides, we had a boat booked.

That night in the hotel by the lakeside when I woke up in horror at what we had done that afternoon, it took me aback. I hadn't expected to react like that. On the boat, we were talking about their lives, looking out at the shores they would have walked on their honeymoon, waiting for the right spot, then asking for the engine to be shut down alongside Wild Cat Island. We said a prayer then lifted the urns, Mum first, then Dad, and dropped them over the side. We joked that Dad's was much heavier, that he would have wanted to 'make a splash'. Mum's was so light, she had worn so thin towards the end, that we thought it might not sink. Then in the night, a sudden dread that we had spilt them, their urns of ashes like a final trace, the essence of their bodies, to be guarded, locked away in a bank vault, cryogenically frozen in a secure facility, future-proofed. And now, all I could think of was their clouds of ash, spreading and thinning to nothing. As if I should have jumped in after them and tried to sift them out, regathered them.

—

It is easy to characterise Simone Weil as a walking act of will, a mind on legs. Those who knew her give the lie to this. There's a story in David McLellan's biography I like, from those final months in London before the sanatorium. She went out with her friend Simone Deitz for an afternoon of boating on the Serpentine. Perhaps sensing Deitz's discomfort at the deep water beneath them, Weil began to rock the boat, teasing the other Simone, rocking and teasing and rocking until finally she tipped them both into the lake.

—

As an atheist student, intent on attacking the irrationality of religious belief whenever I could pick an argument, *Quatuor pour la fin du temps* was an unlikely passion. Messiaen did not play the games of obfuscation favoured by many artists, writers and musicians who have private faith but are worried about narrowing or skewing the reception of their work. I've done some of that obfuscating myself, talking about 'faith and doubt' or 'wrestling with belief'. At times I hear the cock crow. Mostly I tell myself it's justified by the fact that although I lost my atheism in my twenties, I still have some atheist bones. There are days when my doubts harden into disbelief, but always with the caveat that the truth about God is not dependent on whether or not I believe it. Occasionally, though, I am caught unawares and breathless by a sense of the world as full of grace. In those moments the world seems supersaturated with depth, colour, richness, like living inside a William Eggleston photograph or a Frank O'Hara poem.

Grace, and with that grace comes a multiplicity of coincidences, threads that connect everything to everything else. A conviction that in spite of all the horror, the deeper reality is love. In music a 'grace note' means an extra touch, a flourish, not essential to the architecture of the piece. But when Messiaen gives a title like 'Les eaux de la grâce' ('The Waters of Grace') or 'La joie de la grâce' ('The Joy of Grace') he means the opposite. In Christianity, grace is the architecture of everything. It's used to describe the unearned love of God for us, the gift of life and forgiveness and the strength to keep going.

If faith is a gift, then I have been given it, but I know I should be praying for more. I've always thought that the space between faith and doubt, between this world and the possibility of a next, is where poems can be made. It seems to me that the overgrown and tangled territory between sacred and profane (in its original sense of being outside the temple grounds) is where most of the great metaphysical poems were made by the likes of John Donne, Emily Dickinson, George Herbert, Stevie Smith, Blake, Hopkins et al. But Olivier Messiaen is not working in that space between faith and doubt. I like to think he had days, hours, at least moments when he wasn't certain that his God existed. But there's no evidence of such moments in his work. His dots on lines brought about a revolution in modernist music, but it was his words on the page that first got to me. *Quatuor pour la fin du temps* is astonishing enough, but then there are his subtitles for the eight sections of the music, which in English can be rendered in such psychedelic terms as 'Abyss of the Birds', or 'Tangle of Rainbows for the Angel who Announces the End of Time', or 'Praise to the Immortality of Jesus'. This was declarative titling, setting out an unswerving mystical, musical, poetic vision. To me, even then, it was infuriating, intoxicating and irresistible.

I may not listen to the *Quartet* for months now. But I know it will come back. There are poets whose work I'll leave on the shelf for years then pick up and find the same poems changed and made new. A great work of art like *Quatuor pour la fin du temps* can be a goad, guide, punchbag and provocation for a lifetime.

—

Simone Weil's sense that an atheist might be closer to God than a believer, if their atheism arose from a rejection of false pictures of the divine, still has some pull for me. All the pictures of a life beyond the end of time in poetry, painting, films and homilies fall short. I hope there is another encounter, a place beyond place where we can reconnect with those we love. However hard that is to picture, I still find it more persuasive than a full-stop followed by oblivion. I do have faith in eternal life, but it doesn't bear too much thinking about.

Some great poets have gone right up to the border. Henry Vaughan, one of the so-called metaphysical seventeenth-century poets, writing at a time when civil war raged all around him, reckoned up his losses like this: 'They are all gone into the world of light! / And I alone sit ling'ring here'. The reality of death is clear in the poem, as someone finding a bird's nest will know 'at first sight' if the bird is gone, but cannot imagine 'what fair well or grove he sings in now'. And then Vaughan's breathtaking final stanza, addressed directly to the 'Father of eternal life': 'Either disperse these mists, which blot and fill / My perspective still as they pass, / Or else remove me hence unto that hill, / Where I shall need no glass.'

Fascinating as it is to read Jakob Böhme's mystical descriptions of crystalline bodies beyond the end of time, they don't – for this reader – offer any purchase on what eternity may actually entail. The fact that music can summon a world beyond the end of time without figuration or description (if you don't get too distracted by the composer's notes) allows it to bypass the pitfalls of literalism and the limitations of our metaphors. Messiaen's *Quartet*, for this lifelong listener, gets as close as any work of art I know to glimpsing the hill beyond those mists.

—

In Derek Mahon's celebrated poem 'Everything is Going to be All Right', he says 'There will be dying, there will be dying, / but there is no need to go into that.' And in trying to convince himself, he almost convinces you. There is no need to go into it for now, that fact of death, of suffering, but there is need enough to state it, twice, and thereby to bring it into the poem, under a title that fleetingly commands it.

—

PRAISE TO THE IMMORTALITY OF JESUS

There may be no need to go into it, dying, but it's hard not to. Maybe one of the reasons I've gone back to the poems of John Donne all my life is that he goes into it so unflinchingly. In John Stubbs's biography *The Reformed Soul*, there's a story of the poet in his early twenties, when he was a law student in London. It was a time of great religious turmoil and violence, and John Donne, from a Catholic family, had seen close relatives executed for heresy. In the spring of 1593, his younger brother Henry was jailed and died in Newgate Prison. Being sent to Newgate in 1593 was a death sentence. London was in the grip of plague, and in the crowded foul pit of Newgate, infection was pretty much inevitable. There's a passage in Stubbs's biography set in the summer of that plague year, that stuck with me. Bankside, on the south of the river, was a place the young John Donne knew for its theatres and taverns and brothels. But now it had become a ghost town, emptied by terror of the plague. Yet Stubbs describes the young poet wandering through the empty streets, all too aware of the risks he was taking:

> Remaining willingly in town required someone to have more than a slight death wish if there was any chance of escaping. Risking, almost inviting infection, the only recreation for the bilious young writer was either to join in half-hearted legal arguments or go to the bear-pit. It wasn't far from his other haunts on the Bankside. But the show was predictable. Either the bear, chained to a post, was torn apart, or managed to dismember the hounds that were set upon it. There was no other

outcome, and all the animals involved, except the – roaring – spectators, would be maimed by the performance. The sand in the pit went brown and sludged with tattered meat.

It seems too simplistic to say it was entirely in response to the loss of his brother. Of course, his grief was palpable, but this wasn't the only time he put himself in harm's way. There may be a fatalism to it, driven by bereavement and despair, a testing of fate or God by letting go of the guiding hand of caution, the hand that strives to keep you safe.

The same John Donne who as a young man courted death, and witnessed plenty of it, ended up as dean of St Paul's Cathedral in London, leaving us some of the greatest poems in English, plus some astonishing sermons. But that's not all he left. St Paul's has many treasures, but the most striking to me is Nicholas Stone's monument to John Donne. Unlike many effigies, the poet is depicted not flat on his back in eternal repose, but standing, pretty much life-sized. You could stare into his eyes, if his eyes weren't shut. But step back a few paces, and you notice the expression on his face is one of assurance, even love. There's a half-smile on his lips. His hands are clasped in front of him, gathering his grave clothes, his shroud, around him like a blanket. Look down, and you see that he is standing on the lid of his funerary urn. This is a declaration of faith, a declaration of the sort of confidence in the face of death expressed in Psalm 23: 'though I walk through the valley of the shadow of death, I will fear no evil: for thou art with me'.

PRAISE TO THE IMMORTALITY OF JESUS

Izaak Walton, writing several years after Donne's death, claimed that the poet insisted on posing for hours, standing as the model for his own effigy. It might be hard to believe that a sick, old man would be able to do that, but Donne's intention is clear. He wants his effigy to show him not in death, but beyond it. This is a statue of a resurrection body. And every time I stand in front of it, one of his most famous poems comes to mind, one of his Holy Sonnets, which begins with the astonishing lines: 'Death, be not proud, though some have called thee / Mighty and dreadful, for thou art not so'. And ends with the lines: 'One short sleep past, we wake eternally / And death shall be no more; Death, thou shalt die.' Sometimes I read this poem and it seems full of the urbane swagger of Donne, slapping down death like an upstart pupil. But then the defiance comes through. It's thought that Donne came close to dying of a fever around the time he wrote it. Irrespective of the circumstances of its composition, that poem has attitude.

—

Of the many prose poems (I can't stop seeing them in that light, even in translation) from Simone Weil's notebooks, there is one – on the importance of attention and waiting and the role of time – quoted by David McLellan in his biography that stuck with me since the first time I read it: 'God and humanity are like two lovers who have missed their rendezvous. Each is there before the time, but each at a different place, and they wait and wait and wait. He stands motionless, nailed to the spot for the whole of time. She is distraught and impatient. But alas for her, if she gets tired and goes away. For the two places where they are waiting are at the same point in the fourth dimension.' Like Messiaen, Weil believed that God is outside time and we are in it. For her, as McLellan puts it, this means that human beings can only 'disappear into the Divine Presence' by accepting time and whatever necessities come with it.

—

Necessities. Accepting those means – from my reading of Weil – living with and through suffering, grief, loss. But she means more than stoicism or endurance. The toughest parts of her writing, and her life, to read about are those where she seems to embrace, even to love these necessities that come with time.

On the first Friday in Lent, 1622, John Donne preached a sermon in Whitehall on the biblical text John 11:35, the shortest verse in the entire King James Version of the Bible. The verse reads: 'Jesus wept.' He was one year into his role as dean of St Paul's. Having written some of the greatest English love poems, he was now writing some of the greatest metaphysical poems. This is not to suggest that he was one poet who became another. Both were present in his poems from the outset. He had been through five terrible years as a grieving widower and parent. His wife Anne had died shortly after giving birth to a stillborn child. As ever, he's a poet even in his sermon. It is full of riches, but there's one question he asks in it that keeps coming back to me. Picking up on a promise in Revelation about what will happen to us after the end of time, he says: 'And when God shall come to that last act in the glorifying of man, when he promises to wipe all tears from his eyes, what shall God have to do with that eye that never wept?'

—

Three years after his return to Paris from Görlitz, Messiaen was commissioned to write a new piano suite for Christmas which he titled *Vingt regards sur l'enfant-Jésus* (*Twenty Contemplations of the Infant Jesus*). Messiaen began to write the piece in Paris under German occupation in 1944 and finished it in September after liberation. The fact that Marcel Carné was making possibly the greatest French film – *Les Enfants du Paradis* – in occupied Paris at the same time as Messiaen was writing *Vingt regards* made the connection even more compelling.

Like those paintings of the nativity with a ladder or a beam in the background to point to the cross, Messiaen's *Vingt regards* contain the whole story, his longing for the eternity is present even in his celebration of the incarnation's intervention in, and transformation of, time's abyss. I was commissioned to write a set of poems in response to his *Vingt regards*, but as I worked on them, the *Quartet*'s themes crept in too. So did the setting for his composition – occupied Paris – and the fact that even under occupation there were actors, dancers, musicians and directors working and looking to the future.

—

REHEARSAL FOR THE DEATH SCENE

If trees could walk like men,
beautiful boy-god, I would bear you
on my shoulders through this city,
show you every boulevard and alley,
every market stall and park.

You would tower above
the cavalcades and rallies,
peer into penthouse suites and boardrooms,
witness to so many acts of cruelty and love,
safe among my needles.

Then when you nod tired
in the cold and thickening dark
I would stand on the riverbank,
as long slow barges mutter by,
and sing you to sleep in my many tongues:

the bat-high silvered songs
of linden, plane; slow lullabies
of quince and medlar from the gardens;

PRAISE TO THE IMMORTALITY OF JESUS

long laments of empress, foxglove
in the windless squares.

I would carry you for years,
until you grow so heavy that they
nail you up to keep you here. It is needless,
because even if my back broke,
I would never let you fall.

—

I'm woken in the small hours by a tawny owl on Hall Hill. I know it's a tawny owl because it's loud enough to make me reach for my phone and get the app to confirm it. I'd just been reading, in Peter Hill and Nigel Simeone's accounts of Messiaen's birdsong *cahiers*, his notes on a tawny owl he heard one night at his beloved lakeside Pétichet retreat: 'The overall effect is astoundingly bright and wild – it suggests the voice of a woman or a child calling for help – or super-amplified double-bass harmonics . . . the wail and glissando like an ondes martenot or the siren of a boat drawing away into the distance.'

    This morning, from my window, I saw a young, plump male blackbird in the crab apple tree. No song. We are still in its silent months. I think it was in the waiting room for next door's feeders, in a queue behind the jackdaws and magpies, maybe just above the finches in the pecking order. Is it the child of last year's singer? I hope it dodges the neighbourhood cats for long enough to try its voice.

I need to get into Hall Hill soon, when spring comes, to make those recordings of the dawn chorus.

—

I'm trying to work out why it is that after all these years I've never heard the *Quartet* played live. I've had my chances. It crops up not infrequently on concert programmes. I've come to the conclusion that the reason I've never gone to hear it is that I thought it was mine. I knew it wasn't. It is, after all, one of the most lauded musical works of the twentieth century. But my discovery of it in that record shop four decades back felt personal, a gift out of the blue. And almost all my hours spent listening to it have been on my own. If I'd gone to see it live, then would everyone else in the audience think it was theirs too?

Just after lockdown, I was invited to read poems at a live event to be recorded for a broadcast, with poets and musicians sharing the stage. Two of the musicians – violinist Rakhi Singh and pianist Eliza McCarthy – were from the Manchester Collective, known for its innovative programming and performances. After giving a brief introduction to the piece, they played the ravishing fifth movement of the *Quartet*, twin to the eighth and every bit as beautiful. Maybe it was, in part, the fact that we were all – audience and performers – still in that raw state at the end of the pandemic, when it didn't take much to break us down, but I've rarely witnessed a piece of music have such a palpable effect on the people in the room.

PRAISE TO THE IMMORTALITY OF JESUS

Two years on, I see a notice that the Manchester Collective is playing the *Quartet* as part of a tour they're calling 'The End of Time', with the *Quartet* as its centrepiece. The tour finishes back home in the north-west, so I book a ticket to hear the complete *Quatuor pour la fin du temps* played live in the Stoller Hall in Manchester for the first time. There's a programme note that says 'if you're familiar with this work, you know what all the fuss is about. If it's your first time – you've got a hell of a ride ahead of you.'

It was a hell of a ride to the Stoller Hall too. My local stopping train into the city centre stopped too much and got in late, so I took a taxi, only to find much of the city centre cordoned off. The Chanel Show had come to Manchester, with a street in the Northern Quarter turned into a catwalk for the night. Kate Moss (or a lookalike) had been papped in the Ancoats branch of Aldi that morning, rock and movie stars were gathering to look at the frocks paraded by models to a Mancunian playlist of Joy Division, New Order, the Fall. I would have gone out of my way to hear what the late Mark E. Smith made of it all. The city was gridlocked. It was absolutely chucking it down too. I didn't want to get out and walk because the rain was biblical and I'd be sitting in my own steam for *Quartet*.

At the end of the final section, having delivered us into eternity beyond the end of time, the musicians held still and the lights were kept down for what felt like minutes. The hall was full, all ages. At the start, there was a lot of coughing and spluttering (some of it mine) which is no surprise on a wet night in December. By the end we could have held that silence for an hour, two hours.

Nobody wanted to break it. When the lights came on, they were followed by encores and ovations. I felt foolish for waiting all these years to hear the *Quartet* live. There were things I'd never noticed from recordings – the way the clarinet in 'Abîme des oiseaux' can fill a huge hall and make it sound like an abyss, the way some parts I thought were violin were for the cellist and vice versa, the way he doesn't need to bring in an ondes martenot because he can make any instrument become one. But above all, when played as well as this, the way this piece can begin in Stalag VIII-A and end in a vision of eternity so real we can believe it, perhaps even touch it. Back out in the city, the cordons had lifted, the streets were clearing, the rain had dried up.

—

REHEARSAL FOR THE DAY OF JOY

The dancers are stretching, loosening
in their dressing rooms, half made-up

in a mess of costume rails, water-glasses
topped with a dusting of rouge.

Although it's still too soon to dance,
look at the rush of guttered rain through grids

to join the surge towards an open sea.
See how the dry leaves catch in corners,

PRAISE TO THE IMMORTALITY OF JESUS

petals of a burnt manifesto
caught in a breeze between tenements.

And after curfew watch our flags
lift in unison like unbowed heads to mock us,

because the dance, though fugitive, is here,
and will not be held back.

Already it breaks on the roofs of our mouths
and we can barely contain the taste.

It is there in the off-key buskers, dog-howls,
click of the heels of those uniformed men

who think they hold this city captive still,
and soon must think again.

Bibliography

POETRY

Jason Allen-Paisant – *Thinking with Trees* (Carcanet, 2021)

W. H. Auden – *Collected Poems*, ed. Edward Mendelson (Faber & Faber, 1976)

W. H. Auden – *A Certain World: A Commonplace Book* (Faber & Faber, 1982)

John Berryman – *The Dream Songs* (Faber & Faber, 2001)

Elizabeth Bishop – *Poems* (Chatto & Windus, 2011)

Lord Byron – *Poetical Works* (1979)

Anne Carson – *Wrong Norma* (Jonathan Cape, 2024)

Emily Dickinson – *The Poems of Emily Dickinson*, ed. Thomas H. Johnson (Belknap Press, 1955)

John Donne – *The Complete English Poems* (1971)

John Donne – *The Sermons of John Donne* (2004)

T. S. Eliot – *Collected Poems 1909 – 1962* (Faber & Faber, 2002)

Seamus Heaney – *New Selected Poems 1988 – 2013* (Faber & Faber, 2015)

David Jones – *In Parenthesis* (1937)

David Jones – *The Anathemata* (1952)

Patrick Kavanagh – *Collected Poems*, ed. Antoinette Quinn (Allen Lane, 2004)

John Keats – *The Complete Poems* (2006)

Philip Larkin – *The Complete Poems of Philip Larkin* (Faber & Faber, 2014)
Denise Levertov – *New Selected Poems* (Bloodaxe Books, 2003)
Louis MacNeice – *Poems* (Faber & Faber, 1935)
Derek Mahon – *The Poems: 1961 – 2020* (The Gallery Press, 2021)
John Milton – *Paradise Lost* (first published 1667)
Marianne Moore – *New Collected Poems of Marianne Moore* (Faber & Faber, 2021)
Alfred Lord Tennyson – *Poems & Plays* (1983)
Edward Thomas – *Complete Poems* (1969)
Francis Thompson – *The Hound of Heaven* (1986)
William Carlos Williams – *Paterson* (1946)
W. B. Yeats – *Collected Poems* (1982)

EVERYTHING ELSE

Fay Bound Alberti – *This Mortal Coil: The Human Body in History and Culture* (Oxford University Press, 2016)
Jakob Böhme – *Genius of the Transcendent: Mystical Writings of Jakob Böhme*, trans. Jeff Bach and Michael L. Birkel (Shambhala, 2010)
Dietrich Bonhoeffer – *Letters and Papers from Prison*, trans. Reginald Fuller, Frank Clark, John Bowden and others (SCM Press, 2017)
Stephen Broad – *Olivier Messiaen: Journalism 1935 – 1939* (Routledge, 2012)
Richard D. E. Burton – *Olivier Messiaen: Texts, Contexts, and Intertexts (1937 – 1948)* (Oxford University Press, 2016)
Judith Crispin – *Olivier Messiaen: The Centenary Papers* (Cambridge Scholars Publishing, 2011)
Katherine Davies and Toby Garfitt – *God's Mirror: Renewal and Engagement in French Catholic Intellectual Culture in the Mid-Twentieth Century* (Fordham University Press, 2014)

BIBLIOGRAPHY

Simone de Beauvoir – *A Very Easy Death*, trans. Patrick O'Brian (Penguin Classics, 2013)

Christopher Dingle – *The Life of Messiaen* (Cambridge University Press, 2007)

Eamon Duffy – *Faith of our Fathers* (Continuum, 2004)

T. S. Eliot – *The Sacred Wood* (first published 1920)

Delphine Evans – 'Messiaen and the Songs of Wild Birds' (British Library blog, posted 6 December 2016)

Paul Griffiths – *Olivier Messiaen and the Music of Time* (notes on *Quartet* from the booklet with Deutsche Grammophon 'Olivier Messiaen Complete Edition')

Tonino Guerra – 'Stalker, Smuggler of Happiness' in *Andrei Tarkovsky Interviews*, ed. John Gianvito (University Press of Mississippi, 2006)

John Haffenden – *Viewpoints: Poets in Conversation with John Haffenden* (Faber & Faber, 1981)

Peter Hill (ed.) – *The Messiaen Companion* (Faber & Faber, 1994)

Peter Hill and Nigel Simeone – *Messiaen* (Yale University Press, 2005)

Robert Hughes – *The Architects: Louis Kahn* (New Word City, Inc., 2015)

David Jones – *Epoch and Artist: Selected Writings* (Chilmark Press, first published 1959)

D. H. Lawrence – *Lady Chatterley's Lover* (first published 1928)

Julian of Norwich – *Revelations of Divine Love* (first published 1670)

Ludwig Koch – *Memoirs of a Birdman* (Phoenix House, 1955)

Ludwig Koch and E. M. Nicholson – *Songs of Wild Birds* (H. F. & G. Witherby, 1936)

Wendy Lesser – *You Say to Brick: The Life of Louis Kahn* (Farrar, Straus and Giroux, 2017)

Clare Mac Cumhaill and Rachael Wiseman – *Metaphysical Animals:*

How Four Women Brought Philosophy Back to Life (Chatto & Windus, 2022)

Cormac McCarthy – *The Road* (Alfred A. Knopf, 2006)

David McLellan – *Simone Weil: Utopian Pessimist* (Palgrave Macmillan, 1989)

Anthony Pople – *Messiaen: Quatuor Pour la fin du temps* (Cambridge University Press, 1998)

Lawrence M. Principe and Andrew Weeks – 'Jacob Böhme's Divine Substance *Salitter*: its Nature, Origin, and Relationship to Seventeenth Century Scientific Theories' (*British Journal for the History of Science* 22:1, March 1989, pp55 – 61)

Rebecca Rischin – *For the End of Time: The Story of the Messiaen Quartet* (Cornell University Press, 2003)

Claude Samuel – *Olivier Messiaen: Music and Color* (Amadeus Press, 1994)

Cécile Sauvage – *Le Vallon: Poèmes* (Forgotten Books, 2020)

Robert Sherlaw Johnson – *Messiaen* (Dent, 1975)

Galen Strawson – 'A Fallacy of our Age' (TLS, 2004; later republished as 'Against Narrativity')

Seán Street – *Sound at the Edge of Perception: The Aural Minutiae of Sand and other Worldly Murmurings* (Palgrave Pivot, 2018)

Seán Street – *The Sound of a Room: Memory and the Auditory Presence of Place* (Routledge, 2020)

Seán Street – *Wild Track: Sound, Text and the Idea of Birdsong* (Bloomsbury, 2023)

John Stubbs – *Donne: The Reformed Soul* (Penguin, 2006)

Junichiro Tanizaki – *In Praise of Shadows*, trans. Thomas J. Harper and Edward G. Seidensticker (Leete's Island Books, Inc., 1977)

Andrei Tarkovsky – *Sculpting in Time: Reflections on the Cinema* (University of Texas Press, 1989)

BIBLIOGRAPHY

Andrei Tarkovsky – *Time within Time: The Diaries 1970 – 1986* (Faber and Faber, 1994)

Andrei Tarkovsky – *Tarkovsky: Films, Stills, Polaroids & Writings* (Distributed Art Publishers, 2019)

Simone Weil – *On Science, Necessity and the Love of God*, trans. Richard Rees (Oxford University Press, 1968)

Simone Weil – *Oppression and Liberty*, trans. A. Wills and J. Petrie (Virago Press, 1986)

Simone Weil – *Seventy Letters: Personal and Intellectual Windows on a Thinker*, trans. Richard Rees (Wipf and Stock, 2015)

Simone Weil – *Selected Essays, 1934 – 1943: Historical, Political, and Moral Writings* (Wipf and Stock, 2015)

Simone Weil – *The Notebooks of Simone Weil*, trans. Arthur Wills (Routledge & Kegan Paul, 1956)

Acknowledgements

I'm very grateful to Iwan Russell-Jones, Felix Sprang, Helga Schwalm, James MacMillan, Emily Howard, Kate Romano, Seán Street, Martin Bence, Jane Shaw, Philip Archer and Jean Sprackland for conversations, correspondence and companionship on some of this book's travels, to the curators and guides and musicians, especially guides Alexandra Grochowski and Klaudyna Michalska at Meetingpoint Memory Messiaen and the European Centre of Education and Culture in Görlitz, to Dr Markus Ritz the ornithologist and to all the musicologists and Messiaen scholars whose work helped me to get under the skin of this remarkable piece of music. Earlier versions of the sections on Pluscarden Abbey and Waco appeared in *Granta* and *Poetry Review* and some of the material on Tennyson in an essay for the *Anglistentag*. I'm grateful to the producers and commissioners for the opportunity to explore some of these ideas in broadcasts and other projects – especially to Michael Wakelin, Geoff Bird, Susan Roberts, Faith Lawrence, Jeremy Grange, Nadia Molinari, Cordelia Williams, Artangel. My work on this book was supported by an

ACKNOWLEDGEMENTS

Authors Foundation Award from the Society of Authors and by my colleagues in Arts and Humanities research at Manchester Metropolitan University. I'm greatly indebted to my editors – Robin Robertson for the original commission and Bea Hemming for invaluable discussions, trust and faith as the proposal developed into a different book; to the wider teams at Cape and Vintage; to my agent Anna Webber, as ever, for all her wise counsel; to Caroline Hawkridge for essential work on setting up trips and permissions. My last words of gratitude must go to my family: Ruth, Joe, Paddy and Griff, my sister Deb and Iris and David – for everything.

The epigraph, translated from a Messiaen quotation, is taken from Iain G. Matheson's essay 'The End of Time: a Biblical Theme in Messiaen's *Quatuor*' in *The Messiaen Companion* edited by Peter Hill, published by Faber and Faber.

Quoted translations of Messiaen's introductions to his work are from publications by Rebecca Rischin, Antony Pople and Paul Griffiths, cited in the bibliography.

Quotations from Revelation are from the Authorised Version of the Bible.

My own quoted poems come from the following collections:

From *Ransom* by Michael Symmons Roberts published by Jonathan Cape. Copyright © Michael Symmons Roberts, 2021. Reprinted by permission of The Random House Group Limited.

From *Drysalter* by Michael Symmons Roberts published by Jonathan Cape. Copyright © Michael Symmons Roberts,

ACKNOWLEDGEMENTS

2013. Reprinted by permission of The Random House Group Limited.

From *Mancunia* by Michael Symmons Roberts published by Jonathan Cape. Copyright © Michael Symmons Roberts, 2017. Reprinted by permission of The Random House Group Limited.

From *Corpus* by Michael Symmons Roberts published by Jonathan Cape. Copyright © Michael Symmons Roberts, 2004. Reprinted by permission of The Random House Group Limited.

From *Soft Keys* by Michael Symmons Roberts published by Jonathan Cape. Copyright © Michael Symmons Roberts, 1993. Reprinted by permission of The Random House Group Limited.

Excerpts from 'Musée des Beaux Arts', 'Lullaby', 'Bucolics II: Woods' and 'Horae Canonicae' from *Collected Poems* by W. H. Auden and excerpt from *A Certain World: A Commonplace Book* by W. H. Auden, Copyright © 1939, 1940, 1952, and 1955 by The Estate of W. H. Auden. Reprinted by permission of Curtis Brown, Ltd. All rights reserved.

Excerpt from *Wrong Norma* by Anne Carson published by Jonathan Cape. Copyright © Anne Carson, 2024. Reprinted by permission of The Random House Group Limited.

Excerpt from 'Listen' by Jason Allen-Paisant (*Thinking with Trees*, 2021) is reprinted by permission of Carcanet Press, UK.

Excerpt from 'Everything Is Going to Be All Right' by Derek Mahon from *The Poems: 1961 – 2020* (2021). www.gallerypress.com

ACKNOWLEDGEMENTS

Excerpt from 'Days' by Philip Larkin from *The Complete Poems of Philip Larkin*, is reprinted by permission of Faber and Faber Ltd.

Excerpt from 'St Kevin and the Blackbird' by Seamus Heaney from *New and Selected Poems 1988 – 2013*, is reprinted by permission of Faber and Faber Ltd.

Excerpts from 'Four Quartets' and 'Ash Wednesday' from *Collected Poems* by TS Eliot 1909-1962 is reprinted by permission of Faber and Faber Ltd.

Excerpts from 'Because I could not stop for Death' from *The Poems of Emily Dickinson* edited by Thomas H. Johnson, Cambridge, Mass.: The Belknap Press of Harvard University Press, Copyright © 1951, 1955 by the President and Fellows of Harvard College. Copyright © renewed 1979, 1983 by the President and Fellows of Harvard College. Copyright © 1914, 1918, 1919, 1924, 1929, 1930, 1932, 1935, 1937, 1942, by Martha Dickinson Bianchi. Copyright © 1952, 1957, 1958, 1963, 1965, by Mary L. Hampson. Used by permission. All rights reserved.

Excerpt of 'Snow' from *Poems* by Louis MacNeice © Louis MacNeice, 1935, published by Faber and Faber, reproduced by kind permission by David Higham Associates, UK

Excerpt of 'Advent' from *Collected Poems* by Patrick Kavanagh, 2004, published by Allen Lane, reproduced by kind permission of Jonathan Williams Literary Agency, Ireland

Excerpt of 'What are Years?' from *New Collected Poems of Marianne Moore* by Marianne Moore, 2021, is reprinted by permission of Faber and Faber Ltd, UK

Excerpts from 'Dream Song #14' "Life, friends" from

ACKNOWLEDGEMENTS

The Dream Songs by John Berryman © 1969 by John Berryman. Copyright renewed 1997 by Kate Donahue Berryman. Reprinted by permission of Faber & Faber Limited and Farrar, Straus and Giroux. All Rights Reserved.

Excerpt of section 4 of 'The Showings: Lady Julian of Norwich, 1342 – 1416' from *New Selected Poems* by Denise Levertov, 2003, reproduced by kind permission of Bloodaxe Books, UK

Excerpt from 'The Fish' from *Poems* by Elizabeth Bishop published by Chatto & Windus © The Alice H. Methfessel Trust, 2011. Reprinted by permission of The Random House Group Limited

Messiaen's 'cahiers' are held by the Olivier Messiaen and Yvonne Loriod Fund 1900-2010, Bibliothèque Nationale de France (BnF), Département de la Musique. Paris. I am grateful to Dr Marie-Gabrielle Soret and to Professor Thomas Lacôte.

The BBC's lockdown showing of Uncle Vanya, by Anton Chekhov in a new version written by Conor McPherson was filmed in the (then empty) Harold Pinter Theatre in London and directed by Ian Rickson.